THE VISUAL
DICTIONARY *of*
EVERYDAY
THINGS

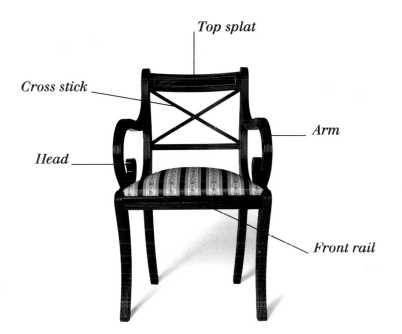

Top splat

Cross stick

Arm

Head

Front rail

FRONT VIEW OF CHAIR

Intermediate ring

Reel seat

Screw locking nut

Tip ring

Butt cap

Hand grip

FLY ROD

Escape wheel

Pinion

Third wheel

Center wheel

INTERNAL WORKINGS OF CLOCK

Winding key

Cradle switch

Earpiece

Base

Handset

EXTERNAL VIEW OF TELEPHONE

Hub

Spoke

Rim

Inner tube

Tongue

Cuff

Vamp

Counter

Wing cap

CRENSON 6154/19 .7/EX

Valve

Outsole

CROSS SECTION OF FINISHED SHOE

Heel

Tire

FRONT WHEEL

EYEWITNESS VISUAL DICTIONARIES

THE VISUAL
DICTIONARY *of*
EVERYDAY
THINGS

Ribbon

Platen

Bail arm

Platen knob

Line spacing
lever

Top plate

Type bar

EXTERNAL VIEW OF TYPEWRITER

DORLING KINDERSLEY
LONDON • NEW YORK • STUTTGART

A DORLING KINDERSLEY BOOK

Project Art Editor Ross George
Designer Johnny Pau
Design Assistant Lesley Betts

Project Editors Tim Fraser, Stephanie Jackson, Paul Docherty
Researcher Clive Webster

Series Art Editor Paul Wilkinson
Art Director Chez Picthall
Managing Editor Ruth Midgley

Photography Dave King, Steve Gorton, Tim Ridley

Production Hilary Stephens

Front hackle

Tail

Head

Wing

DEER HOPPER DRY FLY

First American Edition, 1991

10 9 8 7 6 5 4

Dorling Kindersley, Inc., 95 Madison Avenue
New York, New York 10016

ISBN: 1-879431-17-3 (Trade edition)
ISBN: 1-879431-32-7 (Library Edition)

Library of Congress Card Catalog Number: 91-60898

Reproduced by GRB Grafica, Verona, Italy
Printed and bound in Italy by Arnoldo Mondadori, Verona

Contents

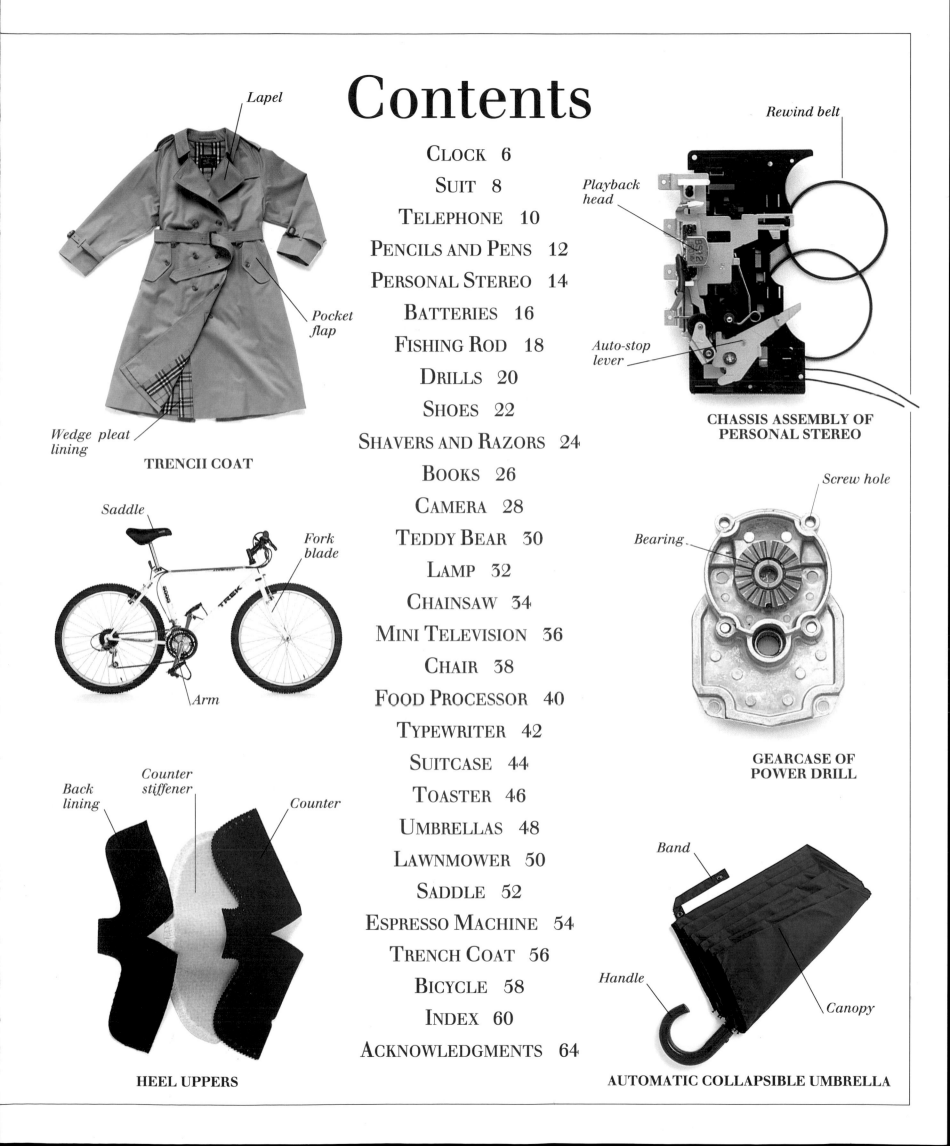

Lapel

Pocket flap

Wedge pleat lining

TRENCH COAT

Saddle

Fork blade

Arm

Back lining

Counter stiffener

Counter

HEEL UPPERS

Rewind belt

Playback head

Auto-stop lever

CHASSIS ASSEMBLY OF PERSONAL STEREO

Screw hole

Bearing

GEARCASE OF POWER DRILL

Band

Handle

Canopy

AUTOMATIC COLLAPSIBLE UMBRELLA

CLOCK 6

SUIT 8

TELEPHONE 10

PENCILS AND PENS 12

PERSONAL STEREO 14

BATTERIES 16

FISHING ROD 18

DRILLS 20

SHOES 22

SHAVERS AND RAZORS 24

BOOKS 26

CAMERA 28

TEDDY BEAR 30

LAMP 32

CHAINSAW 34

MINI TELEVISION 36

CHAIR 38

FOOD PROCESSOR 40

TYPEWRITER 42

SUITCASE 44

TOASTER 46

UMBRELLAS 48

LAWNMOWER 50

SADDLE 52

ESPRESSO MACHINE 54

TRENCH COAT 56

BICYCLE 58

INDEX 60

ACKNOWLEDGMENTS 64

Clock

MECHANICAL CLOCKS HAVE TWO essential elements: a mainspring and a pendulum. When the clock is wound with the key, the mainspring is tightened. As the mainspring unwinds, it turns the gears, which move the minute and hour hands at different speeds around the face of the clock. The pendulum ensures that the hands move at a regular pace. At the top of the pendulum are two hooks called pallets. As the pendulum swings, the pallets allow the escape wheel to turn slowly and evenly.

CLOCK CASE

Steady pin hole

Screw hole

Pallet arbor position

Barrel pivot hole

Wood peg

Fusee pivot hole

Pillar

Ratchet screw

Ratchet pawl

Click wheel

Winding key

Barrel arbor hook

PENDULUM ASSEMBLY

Mainspring barrel arbor

Pallet cock screw

Pallet cock

CLOCK TRAIN

Pallet arbor

Pallet screw

Crutch screw

Pallet

Suspension spring

Crutch

Escape wheel

Mainspring barrel cap

Pinion

FRONT PLATE

Mainspring

Third wheel

Pendulum rod

Pinion

Pinion

Center wheel

Fusee

Mainspring barrel

Fusee chain

Pivot hole

Lenticular bob

Fusee stop screw

Fusee stop

Tension spring screw

Tension spring

Rating nut

Side inspection door

Wood peg

Back plate

Bottom door key

Back box

Bottom door

Minute hand

Screw hole

Minute wheel cock

Cock screw

Minute wheel

Dial washer

Hour hand screw

Hand collet

Cannon pinion

Pin

Hour wheel

Bridge

Bridge screw

Pin

Dial foot hole

Pillar hole

CLOCK FACE

Wood bezel

Hinged brass bezel

Minute track

Hour marker

Roman numeral

CAMERER. KUSS & C°.
56 New Oxford St

Maker's name

Center hole

Winding hole

Dial

LONDON

Hour hand

7

Suit

A MAN'S TWO-PIECE SUIT IS A SET OF JACKET AND PANTS made in the same material; a three-piece suit has a vest as well. Many design details of modern suits hark back to previous centuries; for example, the vents at the back of a jacket made the garment hang better while the wearer was horseback riding. Suits are sold either ready-made or made-to-measure (known as bespoke). For a bespoke suit, the customer chooses the style and the cloth and the tailor measures the customer carefully. The tailor then makes up a pattern to these measurements and uses it as a guide for cutting the numerous pieces of fabric and lining needed for the suit.

JACKET

Top collar

Jacket hanger

Back

Stay tape

Forepart

Canvas

Lap hair

Back lining

Padding

Tailor tack

Brace button

Fastening

PANTS

Belt loop

Lining

Right leg back

RIGHT SLEEVE

Shoulder pad

Sleeve head wadding

Top sleeve

Facing of lapel

INSIDE POCKET

Forepart lining

Lining

Under sleeve

Pocket flap and lining

Lining

Pocket lining

Cuff lining

Coin pocket

Right leg front

Cuff button facing

SIDE POCKET

Pocket jet facing

Cuff button

Stay tape

Pocket facing

Pocket lining

COLLAR
- Collar canvas
- Undercollar
- Back

Stay tape

BREAST POCKET
- Pocket welt
- Lining
- Forepart lining
- Back lining

TWO-PIECE SUIT
- Notched lapel
- Hip flap pocket
- Facing of lapel
- Lap hair
- Padding
- Canvas
- Stay tape

Forepart

WAISTBAND
- Back curtain
- Trouser clasp
- Facing
- Left leg front
- Left leg back
- Fly button
- Facing
- Canvas

Pocket jet

Button

French bearer

Material

Pocket flap and lining

LEFT SLEEVE
- Sleeve head wadding
- Jacket button
- Shoulder pad
- Lining
- Top sleeve
- Under sleeve
- Cuff lining
- Lining
- Cuff button facing
- Cuff button
- Gimp

HIP POCKET
- Pocket jet
- Pocket facing
- Lining

Pocket jet facing

SIDE POCKET
- Stay tape
- Pocket facing
- Button hole silk

9

Telephone

A TELEPHONE MAKES IT POSSIBLE TO TALK to someone far away. It works by changing the voice's sound waves into electrical signals that travel very quickly along wires to another telephone. Each telephone has its own number, and to send a signal to someone you either dial their number or press the buttons on the key pad. When a signal arrives at a phone, it activates the tone ringer and this indicates that there is a call waiting to be answered. To talk to someone, you speak into the mouthpiece. The sound waves of your voice vibrate a thin metal disk inside the microphone, and this alters the electrical signal. When the signal reaches the other person's telephone, it travels along wires to an electromagnet in the receiver. The electromagnet moves a diaphragm which vibrates the surrounding air so that it sounds like the caller's voice.

Screw

Rubber sealing washer

Earpiece transducer

Dustcover for earpiece

Keypad membrane

PUSH BUTTON KEY PAD

Decorative plastic trim

Earpiece

Screw

Keytop

Printed circuit board

Window

Redial button

Carbon contact

Memory button

Key pad casing

Dustcover for mouthpiece

Screw

Screw

Handset front cover

Number list

Top casing

TELEPHONE HANDSET

Screw

Mouthpiece

Screw

PRINTED CIRCUIT BOARD

Integrated circuit

Resistor

Transistor

Integrated circuit

Ribbon
cable

Resistor

Keypad
contact

Capacitor

Wire

Socket

Microphone

Retaining screw

Handset back
cover

Cradle
switch

Base

Handset
cord plug

Hand-
set

Cord

Handset cord

Printed circuit
board

TELEPHONE BASE

Piezo tone
ringer

Solder
joint

Ringer
on/off switch

Rubber
foot back

Handset
cord

Telephone
cord

Wire

Base casing

Exchange
number

Handset cord plug

Diode

Wire

Telephone cord plug

Cradle switch
assembly

Return spring

Hole for
cradle switch

Cradle switch
lever

Screw

Washer

Pencils and pens

PENCILS AND PENS ARE USED for writing and drawing. Pencils have the advantage that any mistakes can be easily rubbed out. We commonly call them "lead pencils" but this term is a misnomer because the main ingredient of the "lead" is graphite, a form of carbon. The graphite is mixed with clay and fired in an oven; the more clay a pencil has, the paler the line drawn. In simple pencils the lead is encased in a wood stick that has to be sharpened. Mechanical pencils have metal or plastic cases; when you press the cap, or twist the tip of the cap, the lead appears. Fountain pens have a reservoir that holds ink and a nib through which ink flows on to the paper. When you use a fountain pen, the width of the nib, the pressure you exert, and the consistency of the ink all affect the thickness of the line drawn. Ballpoint pens are less versatile but generally more popular because they are easier to use. When you write or draw with a ballpoint pen, a ball in the nib rotates, allowing a small amount of thick ink to ooze out.

TYPES OF PENCILS AND PENS

Wood

Lead

Lead guard

GRAPHITE (LEAD) PENCIL

Clip

Nose

Tassie

MECHANICAL PENCIL

Outer cap

Barrel

FOUNTAIN PEN

Clip

Over cap

BALLPOINT PEN

GRAPHITE (LEAD) PENCIL

Wood

Graphite

MECHANICAL PENCIL

Eraser

Cleaning wire

Clutch

Plug

Cap

Clip

Lead

Spring

Barrel

Lead tube

Collet retainer

Spring

Metal collet

Nose

Lead guard

FOUNTAIN PEN

Tassie screw

Clip

Outer cap

Nib

Inner cap

Feed

Spring

Collector

Filler unit (converter)

Clutch

Piercer tube

Collector shell

Connector

Barrel band

Filler unit

Barrel

Tassie

Clip screw bush

Clip screw

BALLPOINT PEN

Clip screw

Clip

Over cap

Connector

Barrel

Collector

Nib

Spring

BALLPOINT

Spring

Ink tube

Nib

Bull

NIB

Iridium tip

Tine

Slit

Eye (piercing)

Wing

Wing

Heel

Personal stereo

A PERSONAL STEREO IS A SMALL, BATTERY-POWERED, portable cassette player that reproduces sound recorded on magnetic tape. A cassette, holding tape wound on two reels, slots into the machine so that the reels fit over two spindles. Pressing the "play" button causes a pinch roller and a capstan to rotate and drive the tape over the playback head, while the reels supply the tape and take up the slack. A magnetic pattern, representing sound, is recorded onto the tape. When the playback head comes into contact with the tape, a weak electric current is induced in it by the pattern. The current, which becomes weaker or stronger as the pattern varies, is sent through an amplifier and then to the earphones. In each earphone, the current is converted into a magnetic field that vibrates a small cone, and these vibrations produce sound waves. Stereo sound is reproduced by recording two magnetic patterns, or tracks, one for the left and one for the right ear.

Spring

Chassis

Protective battery contact

Right-angle jack

Stereo jack plug

SONY
SPORTS
WM-B52
CASSETTE PLAYER
WALKMAN

Stop button

Fast-forward button

Rewind button

Play button

Cassette window

Date button

Alarm reset button

Volume control

Jointer

Ring seal

Headphone socket packing

Cabinet rear cover

Headphone jack

Wire

Volume control

Motor control integrated circuit

Main integrated circuit

Female lead connector

Tape type selector

Cassette holder click arm assembly

Belt clip

Function button seal

Clock

Power indicator

Tape select

Stop button

Fast-forward button

Rewind button

Cassette holder clamper

Carry case

Play button

Tape speed adjustment packing

Main mounted printed circuit board

Motor speed preset

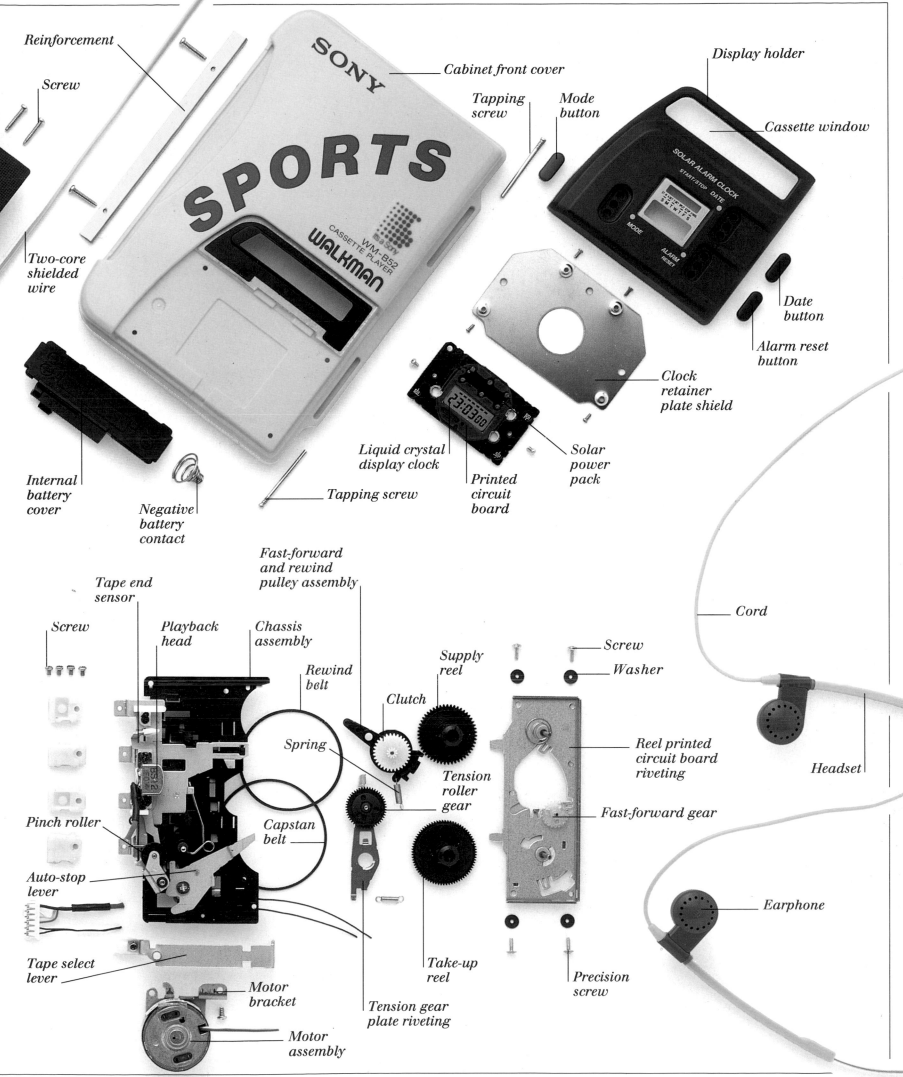

Reinforcement

Screw

Two-core shielded wire

Cabinet front cover

SONY

SPORTS

WALKMAN
CASSETTE PLAYER
WM-B52

Tapping screw

Mode button

Display holder

SOLAR ALARM CLOCK

Cassette window

Date button

Alarm reset button

Clock retainer plate shield

Internal battery cover

Negative battery contact

Liquid crystal display clock

Tapping screw

Printed circuit board

Solar power pack

Cord

Fast-forward and rewind pulley assembly

Tape end sensor

Screw

Playback head

Chassis assembly

Rewind belt

Supply reel

Screw

Washer

Spring

Clutch

Pinch roller

Capstan belt

Tension roller gear

Reel printed circuit board riveting

Headset

Auto-stop lever

Fast-forward gear

Tape select lever

Take-up reel

Earphone

Motor bracket

Tension gear plate riveting

Precision screw

Motor assembly

Batteries

CONVENIENT, PORTABLE SOURCES of electricity are usually known as batteries, although most of them should really be called "power cells." Strictly speaking, a battery is a set of power cells used together. Of the examples shown here, only the car battery is a true battery as it contains several cells in one case. All the others are single power cells. Most batteries, including the commonly used alkaline manganese cells and most button batteries, must be replaced when the chemicals they contain no longer provide electricity. Other batteries, such as nickel-cadmium cells and lead acid car batteries, are rechargeable and can be used over and over again.

HOW A POWER CELL WORKS

All chemical power cells basically consist of two electrodes (anode and cathode) immersed in a chemical powder or liquid called an electrolyte. The anode is connected to the cell's negative terminal, the cathode to the positive terminal. Such cells produce a current by converting chemical energy into electrical energy. When a cell's terminals are connected to form an electrical circuit, an electric current (consisting of a flow of negatively charged particles called electrons) passes through the circuit from the negative to the positive terminal.

ALKALINE MANGANESE POWER CELLS

Steel jacket (cathode collector)

Outer steel jacket

Negative terminal

Direction of electron flow

Positive terminal

Manganese dioxide and graphite cathode

Anode (electrode)

Cathode (electrode)

Electrolyte

LEAD ACID CAR BATTERY

Negative terminal   Positive terminal

Positive terminal   Vent plug

Battery cover

Lead metal negative plate

Cell divider

Plate separator

Lead oxide positive plate

16

POWER CELLS FOR CAMERAS

MERCURY

ALKALINE

LITHIUM

LITHIUM

Separator

RECHARGEABLE NICKEL-CADMIUM POWER CELL

Positive terminal

Insulating seal ring

Resealable vent mechanism

Nickel-plated steel case

"Sandwiched" layers of cadmium anode, separator, and nickel oxide cathode

Positive terminal

Negative terminal

CROSS SECTION OF A BUTTON CELL

Cell top (negative terminal)

Absorbent separator

Anode

Nylon seal

Sleeve

Cathode

Barrier separator

Cell case (positive terminal)

BUTTON CELLS FOR WATCHES AND HEARING AIDS

Zinc air button cell

Plastic grommet

Lithium manganese button cell

Alkaline button cell

Lithium manganese button cell

Vent

F 8

Silver oxide button cell

Air seal

Support ring

Washer

Cathode cap (positive terminal)

Outer steel jacket

Anode collector

Anode cap (negative terminal)

Zinc gel anode

MN1300 LR20 SIZE D 1,5 Volts

DURACELL ALKALINE

Fishing tackle

MANY ANGLERS USE A BEWILDERING variety of tackle, but the fundamental items needed for fishing are a rod, reel, line, and lure. The angler uses the rod, reel, and line to cast the lure over the water. The reel controls the line as it spills off the spool and as it is wound back. Some reels have a gearing system that provides the power for reeling in fighting fish. Weights, sometimes called sinkers or leads, may be attached to the line so that it will sink to the required depth. Swivels are attached to prevent the line from twisting. The lure, whether artificial or real bait, must fool the fish into trying to attack or eat it. Artificial flies often imitate the appearance, movement, and sometimes the scent of the prey on which some fish feed. When a fish bites, the hook must become embedded in its mouth and remain there while the catch is reeled in.

BUTT SECTION

Keeper ring

Drag spindle

Handgrip

Disk drag

Drag washer

Disk spring

Gear retainer

Dual click gear

Retaining screw

Check pawl cover

Check pawl

Check slide

Check spring

REELS

Spool-release button

Reel foot (reel scoop)

Plate-nut

Click mechanism

Mechanical brake

Side plate

Centrifugal brake

Spool

Handle

Level-wind system

Star drag

MULTIPLIER REEL

Line

Unskirted spool

Reel foot (reel scoop)

Handle

Tension nut (drag adjustment)

Ratchet (anti-reverse device)

Handgrip

Reel

Bail arm

FIXED-SPOOL REEL

HOOKS, SWIVELS, AND WEIGHTS

Eye

Shank

ANATOMY OF A HOOK

Gape

Bend

Throat

Point

Barb

TREBLE HOOK

ABERDEEN HOOK

REVERSED BEND HOOK

EXAMPLES OF BARREL SWIVELS

HILLMAN ANTI-KINK WEIGHT

FLY ROD AND REEL

Intermediate ring

TIP SECTION

Reel seat

Screw locking nut

Tip ring

Disk drag housing

Reel foot (reel scoop)

Line

Butt cap

Drag knob screw

Butt extension

Release lever

Spool screw

Clicker plate

DragonFly 100

Disc Drag

Drag knob

ARTIFICIAL FLIES

Line guide

DUNKELD WET FLY

Tail

Body

Cheek

Head

Line guide cover

Hackle

Retaining screw

Ribbing

Release spring

Spool cover

Handle

Spool-release button

ARTIFICIAL LURES

DEVON MINNOW

Fin

Eye

Treble hook

Swivel

Tulip mount

DEER HOPPER DRY FLY

Front hackle

Eye

Tail

Head

Wing

Hook

JOINTED PLUG

Adjustable vane

Joint

Treble hook

Drills

THE ELECTRICALLY POWERED MOTOR OF A POWER DRILL, cooled by a fan, turns a shaft at high speed. The shaft connects, in turn, to a system of gears that rotates a chuck even faster. Clamped by the chuck, a sharp drill bit cuts out the hole, and at the same time the bit's screw-shaped grooves channel the waste out of the hole. For drilling hard materials, many power drills have a hammer mechanism; when this is operated a ratchet in the gearcase causes the chuck and bit to pound in and out as they drill. A hand drill, although slower and less forceful than a power drill, is easier to control. For cutting wide holes, carpenters often prefer a brace-and-bit. This acts like a lever: the bowed handle of the brace moves a larger distance than the bit, turning the bit with extra force.

MOTOR ASSEMBLY

Commutator

Armature

Armature spindle

Fan

Motor case

Field

Motor case

Brush spring

Screw

Washer

Brush

Lead wire to motor

Brush holder

Top insert blank

Hammer mechanism actuator

Screw hole

Electromagnetic induction capacitor

Chuck key holder

Switch

Hammer actuator position

Gearcase position

Motor position

INTERNAL VIEW OF HOUSING COVER

Screw

Lock button

Switch trigger

Trigger position

Washer

Spring

TRIGGER MECHANISM

Cable cordset

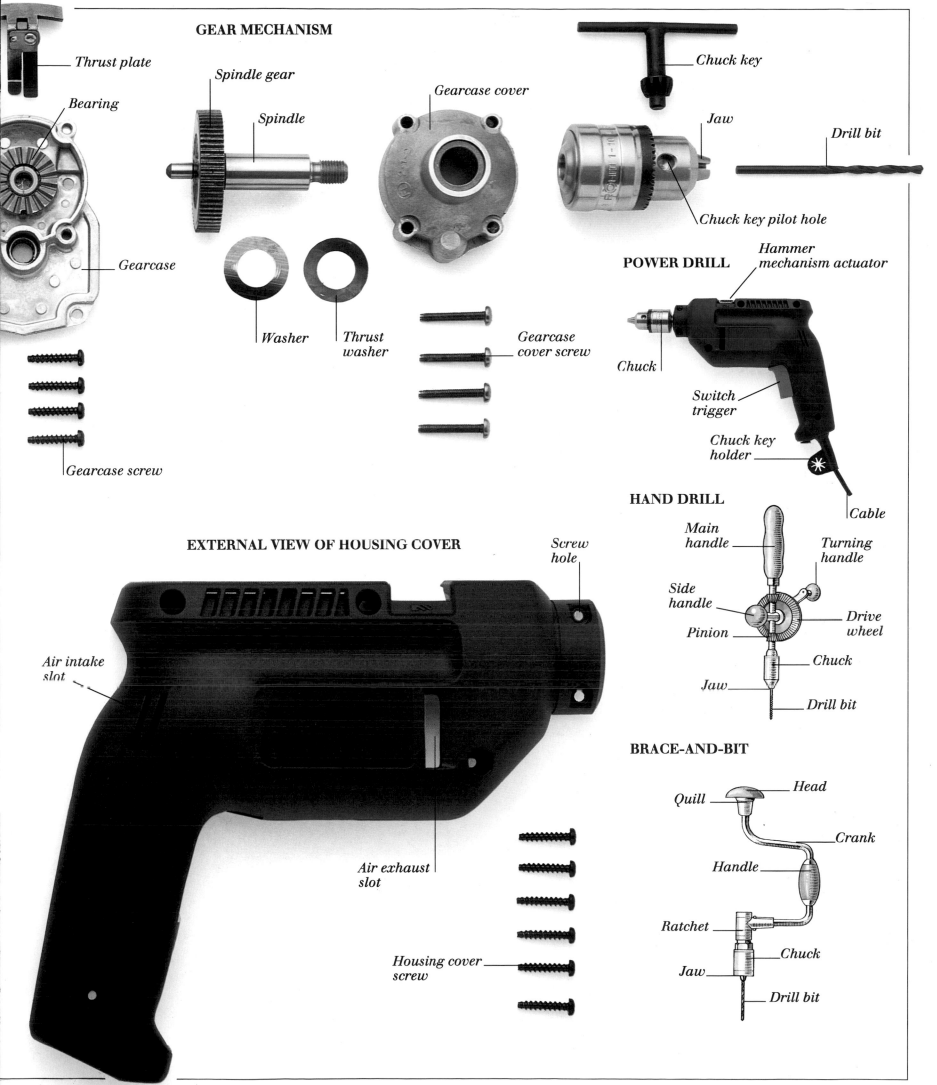

GEAR MECHANISM

Thrust plate

Bearing

Spindle gear

Spindle

Gearcase cover

Chuck key

Jaw

Drill bit

Gearcase

Chuck key pilot hole

Washer

Thrust washer

Gearcase cover screw

POWER DRILL

Hammer mechanism actuator

Chuck

Switch trigger

Chuck key holder

Gearcase screw

Cable

HAND DRILL

Main handle

Turning handle

Side handle

Drive wheel

Pinion

Chuck

Jaw

Drill bit

EXTERNAL VIEW OF HOUSING COVER

Screw hole

Air intake slot

Air exhaust slot

Housing cover screw

BRACE-AND-BIT

Head

Quill

Crank

Handle

Ratchet

Chuck

Jaw

Drill bit

Shoes

WELL MADE SHOES PROTECT THE FEET and are also comfortable and long lasting. The best shoemakers use a wood or plastic mold, called a last, which matches the shape of the customer's foot. The different parts of a shoe are stitched and glued together around the last; rivets and nails are used only in the heel, which is built up from layers of leather and rubber. The steel shank gives support to the arch of the foot and, with the seat lift, helps the wearer maintain posture. The layers of the sole give strength, while the soft insole cushions the foot. The leather welt sewn between the leather uppers and the sole ensures a strong join.

Inside quarter

Quarter lining

Wing cap and vamp backer

Quarter backer

Inner sock

Counter

Tongue

Shoelace

Outside quarter

Vamp

Wing cap

Wing cap backer

Vamp

Box toe

CROSS SECTION OF FINISHED SHOE

Tongue

Tongue lining

Punchhole

Tongue

Cuff

Vamp

Heel grip

Wing cap

Counter

Welt

Welt

Seat lift

Perforated wing cap

Insole

Bottom filler

Outsole

Lining

Steel shank

Heel

GRENSON 6154/19 7/EX

Quarter backer

Outside quarter

Shoelace

Eyelet

Tag

Counter

Counter stiffener

Quarter and counter lining

Cone

LAST

Thimble (jack-locating hole)

Back lining

Vamp backer

Hinge

Bottom filler

Outsole

Shank

Seat lift

Inner sock

Insole with ribbing

Welt

Thread

Quarter tip

Heel nail

Seat rivet

Heel

23

Shavers and razors

ALL SHAVERS AND RAZORS GIVE A SMOOTH shave by cutting hair as close to the skin as possible without causing injury. The most basic razor is a barber's cut-throat, an extremely sharp open blade. The cut-throat has the advantage that it can be resharpened when blunt; a drawback is that it can inflict a serious wound. Because of this danger the safety razor was invented. Its disposable blade is protected by a guard that prevents deep cuts to the skin. Safer still is the electric shaver. The rechargeable one shown here has two blade screen combs in the shaving head, which hold the hairs as the rotating blades, or cutters, cut them, while a sprung drive shaft ensures that the blades cut close to the screen combs. A beardtrimmer, on the side of the shaver, has two serrated blades, one of which slides sideways over the other.

ELECTRIC SHAVER

Blade screen comb

Shaving head holder

Comfort control

On/off switch

Battery level indicator

Charge lamp

Plug socket

GEAR SYSTEM

Gear wheel

Cutter

Bracket

Spring

Blade screen comb

Drive shaft

Washer

Gear wheel

SHAVING HEAD

Protective cap

Shaving head holder

Comfort control

Retaining plate assembly

Release catch

Gear cover

Gear frame

Trimmer operating lever

CUT-THROAT RAZOR

Handle

Pivot

Blade

SAFETY RAZOR

Collar

Handle

Case

Double-edged blade

Guard

OUTER CASE

Side strip panel interior

On/off indicator

Switch position

On/off knob

On/off switch frontplate

On/off switch backplate

Side strip panel exterior

MOTOR

Spring

Rotor

Battery level indicator

Charge lamp

Case exterior

Plug

BEARDTRIMMER

Trimmer release

Trimmer blades

Wire spring

Case screw

Spring

Mains lead

Motor brush assembly

Plug socket

Motor case

Case interior

Screw hole

PHILISHAVE
Tracer

Maker's model and trademark

Transformer

Capacitor

Capacitor

Capacitor

Rectifier

Printed circuit board

Safety fuse resistor

PANEL ASSEMBLY

Rechargeable battery cell

Inlet

Motor lead

Books

THOUGH THE PROCESS OF BOOKBINDING today is usually mechanized, some books are still bound by hand. The pages of a book are printed on large sheets of paper called sections, or signatures. When folded, sections usually make 8, 16, or 32 pages. To assemble a hand-bound hardback book, the binder first places the folded sections in the correct order within the endpapers. Next, he or she sews the sections together along the spine edge using strong thread and then pastes them with glue for extra strength. After trimming the pages, the binder puts the book in a press and hammers the spine to shape it. The binder then glues one or more linings on the spine. The cover, or case, comes last. To make this, the bookbinder sticks cover boards to the endpapers, front and back, and then covers them with cloth or leather.

HALF-BOUND BOOK **LEATHER-BOUND BOOK**

Spine

Corner piece

Tail

Marbleized paper

Joint

Leather cover

Fore edge

Rib

Spine

Ribbon

Tail

Gold tooling

HALF-BOUND BOOK

Marbleized paper

Buckram corner piece

Pastedown (endpaper)

Lining

Mull

Headband

Spine piece

Section (signature)

Tape

Front cover board

Tailband

Manila

LEATHER-BOUND BOOK

Pastedown (endpaper)

Headband

Rib

Tape

Leather cover

Back cover board

Section (signature)

Frontispiece

Thread

Front cover board

Ribbon

Lining

Tailband

Mull

Flyleaf (endpaper)

Buckram corner piece

Back cover board

Reverse of marbleized paper

Buckram corner piece

Pastedown (endpaper)

LEATHER-BOUND BOOK

Joint

Ribbon

Headband

Mull

Tape

Rib

Lining

Spine

Fore edge

Flyleaf (endpaper)

Pastedown (endpaper)

Front cover board

Leather cover

Gold tooling

Camera

A CAMERA IS AN INSTRUMENT used for recording images on photographic film. It consists of a light-tight box with a shutter, a lens containing a diaphragm, and a viewing system. When the shutter is released, the film is exposed to light from the subject that is being photographed. Adjusting the shutter speed alters the time for which the film is exposed to light. The diaphragm, by altering the aperture of the lens, controls the intensity of light entering the camera. The total amount of light entering the camera is called the exposure. The lens focuses the light onto the film. When there is insufficient light to produce an adequate image, a flashgun may be used to give extra light.

FRONT VIEW OF CAMERA

Shutter speed dial

Film rewind/back cover release knob

Shutter release button

Strap lug

Exposure counter

PENTAX K1000

smc PENTAX-A 1:2 50mm

Lens lock release lever

X-flash sync terminal

FRONT BOARD ASSEMBLY

Lens mount

Left body covering

Right body covering

Lens lock release lever

X-flash sync cap

BOTTOM COVER ASSEMBLY

Tripod socket hole

Bottom cover

Battery

Battery chamber cap

REAR VIEW OF CAMERA

Film rewind crank

Viewfinder eyepiece

Film take-up spool

Film rewind/back cover release knob

Film roller

Film chamber

Back cover

Film pressure plate

Film rail

Film guide rail

Shutter curtain

Film sprocket spool

LENS BARREL ASSEMBLY

Ornament ring

Cover frame

Nameplate ring

Front lens frame retainer plate

Front lens group

Installing ring retainer plate

Retainer screw

smc PENTAX-A 1:2 50mm

Washer

Retainer screw

Retainer screw

Retainer screw

TOP COVER ASSEMBLY

Shutter dial knob spring
Film speed indicator
Speed dial knob
Shutter speed dial
Retainer screw

Counter dial housing
Film wind lever
Counter dial cover
Exposure counter dial
Wind lever install spring
Wind lever collar
Top cover
X-contact
Hot shoe
Rewind shaft
Film rewind/back cover release knob

Counter dial cover
Retainer screw
Washer
Window
Shutter release button
Shutter speed index
Rewind shaft bushing
Film rewind crank

Prism retainer plate
Prism retainer spring
Cover frame
Retainer screw

MAIN BODY

Viewfinder eyepiece
Pentaprism
Strap lug

Hole for film rewind button

Retainer screw

TOP VIEW OF CAMERA

Focusing ring
Aperture/distance index
Subject distance scale
Depth-of-field guide
Lens alignment node
Aperture auto-lock button
Lens lock release lever
Shutter release button
Shutter cocked indicator
Exposure counter

Film rewind crank
Film rewind/back cover release knob
Hot shoe
X-contact
Shutter speed index
Film speed indicator
Shutter speed dial
Film wind lever

Supporter ring retainer plate
Supporter ring
Diaphragm blade
Installing ring
Main barrel assembly
Rear lens group

Opening and closing plate

Teddy bear

NAMED FOR THE AMERICAN PRESIDENT and dedicated bear hunter, Theodore Roosevelt, the first teddy bear was probably made by a German toymaker, Richard Steiff, at the beginning of this century. Steiff's bear soon became popular because, unlike earlier stuffed bears, its head and limbs were movable. The modern teddy shown here is a direct descendant of Steiff's prototype. It is made in six sections: a head, body, two arms, and two legs. For each section, pieces of golden-colored plush mohair are cut out, sewn together, and stuffed with wood wool. Felt forms the pads of the paws and feet. The eyes are made of colored plastic, and the nose and mouth are embroidered. Disks, screws, and washers connect the limbs and head to the body. When this teddy is tilted, it emits a bear-like growl.

Ear

Eye

Nose

Mouth

Leather collar

Brass buckle

Right arm

Left arm

Body

Left paw

Left leg

Right paw

Right leg

Left ear front

Left ear back

Left side of head

Left arm

Safety washer

Screw

Disk

Eye

Front, top, and back of head

Safety washer

Washer

Right ear back

Right ear front

Left arm

Left paw

Eye

Right ear

BODY

Body

Right leg

Right side of head

Right arm

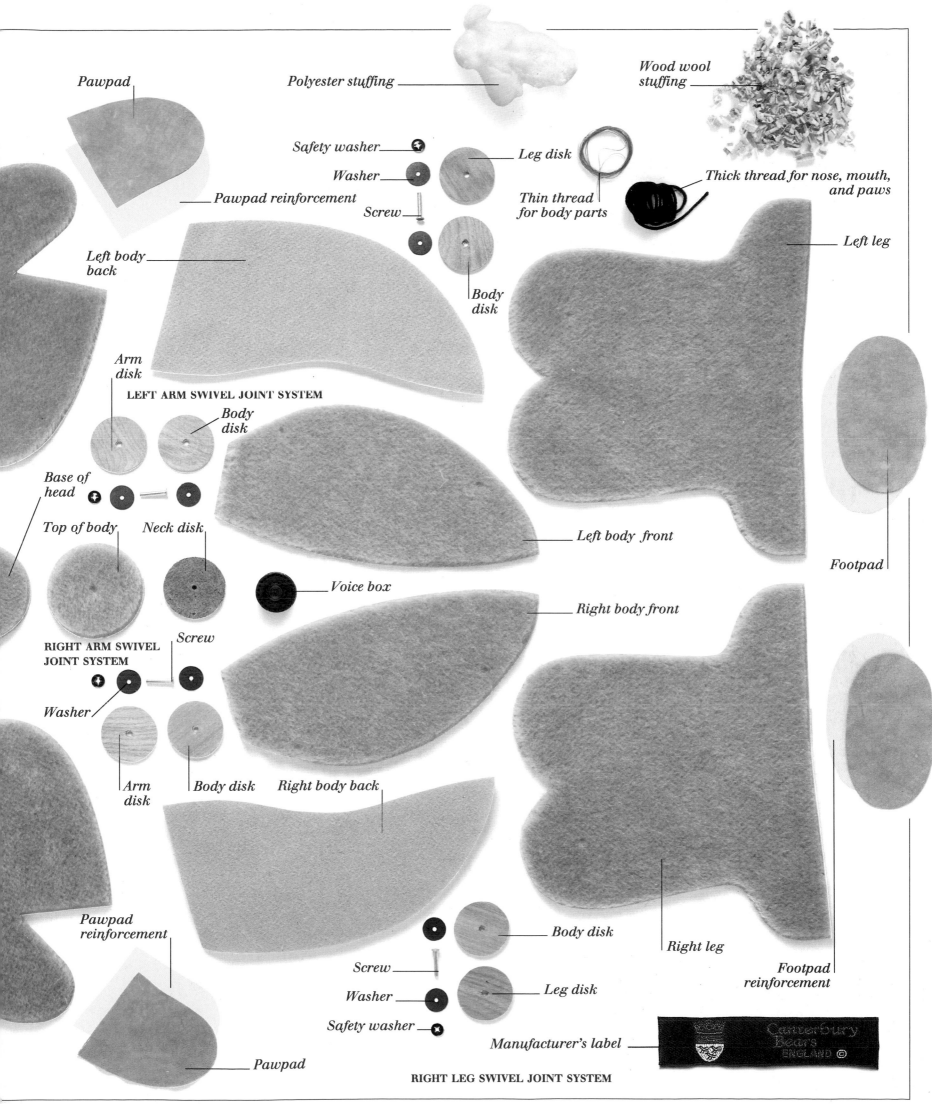

Pawpad

Polyester stuffing

Wood wool stuffing

Safety washer

Washer

Leg disk

Pawpad reinforcement

Thick thread for nose, mouth, and paws

Screw

Thin thread for body parts

Left body back

Left leg

Body disk

Arm disk

LEFT ARM SWIVEL JOINT SYSTEM

Body disk

Base of head

Top of body

Neck disk

Left body front

Voice box

Footpad

Right body front

RIGHT ARM SWIVEL JOINT SYSTEM

Screw

Washer

Arm disk

Body disk

Right body back

Body disk

Right leg

Pawpad reinforcement

Screw

Washer

Leg disk

Safety washer

Manufacturer's label

Canterbury Bears ENGLAND ©

Pawpad

Footpad reinforcement

RIGHT LEG SWIVEL JOINT SYSTEM

Lamp

THE FIRST SPRING-TENSIONED, adjustable work lamp was designed in 1934 by George Carwardine. This type of lamp imitates the human arm in the way that it can be kept in a fixed position or moved easily and precisely. In the arm, such control is achieved by coordinating the opposing action of paired muscles (e.g., when the biceps contracts, the triceps relaxes and the arm bends). In the work lamp, one muscle of a pair is represented by the springs that pull on the rigid bars of the lamp; the other muscle is represented by the nuts, bolts, screws, and washers in the lamp's joints that resist the pull of the springs. By balancing the pull of the springs against the resistance in the joints, the lamp's height and angle can be adjusted with minimal pressure.

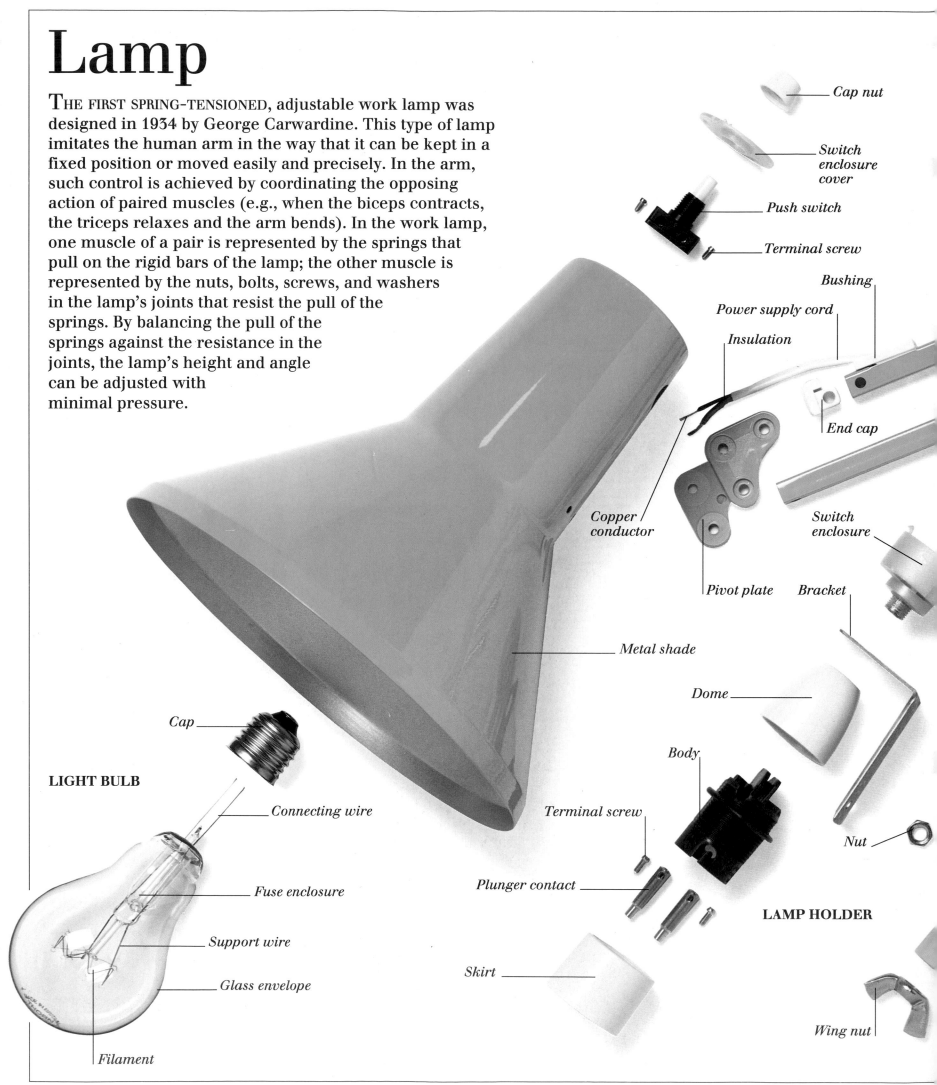

Cap nut

Switch enclosure cover

Push switch

Terminal screw

Bushing

Power supply cord

Insulation

End cap

Copper conductor

Switch enclosure

Pivot plate

Bracket

Metal shade

Dome

Body

LIGHT BULB

Cap

Connecting wire

Terminal screw

Nut

Plunger contact

LAMP HOLDER

Fuse enclosure

Support wire

Skirt

Glass envelope

Wing nut

Filament

SUPPORT ARM ASSEMBLY

Cheese head screw

Washer

Nut

Locking nut

Power supply cord

Pivot plate

End cap

Cheese head screw

Washer

Hexagon nut

Bushing

Metal arm

Spring attachment

Coil tension spring

Clamping screw

Arm coupling

Metal arm

Lamp holder coupling

Pivot

Power supply cord

Spigot

Metal shade

Pivot plate

Shade coupling

Socket

Metal arm

Washer

Spring attachment

Clamp upper jaw

Adjustment locking nut

Coil tension spring

Metal arm

Threaded rod

TABLE CLAMP ASSEMBLY

Coil tension spring

Cheese head screw

Washer

Table clamp

End cap

Nut

Threaded rod

Clamp lower jaw

Spring attachment bolt

Wing nut

33

Chainsaw

A CHAINSAW IS A POWERFUL HAND-HELD tool for chopping wood, and for pruning or cutting down trees. It has a metal chain—similar to a bicycle chain—that moves around a guide bar. Attached to the links of the chain are teeth that cut the wood. Lubricating oil drips continually onto the chain to prevent it from sticking. Chainsaws can be powered by either a gasoline- or an electrically driven motor. The chainsaw shown here has a small gasoline-driven motor, which is started by a recoil rope rotor. This motor rotates a drive cog, or clutch sprocket, which turns the chain. Chainsaws have to perform in all weathers: in hot climates, a fanwheel cools the engine and for cold conditions some models have an electrically heated handle. This tool is potentially dangerous, but hand guards and a chain brake help protect the user from accidents.

Starter grip

Fan housing

Starter rope

Rope rotor

Oil filler cap

Screw

Hexagon nut

Fuel filler cap

Flywheel

Rope

Ignition module

Retainer

Carburetor

Air filter front

Locknut

Control lever

Air filter back

Spark plug

Cylinder

Washer

Self tap screw

E-clip

Shroud

Tank housing

Carburetor box cover

Throttle rod

Rear handle molding

Front handle

Guide bar

Screw

Rope

Retainer

Spiked
bumper

STIHL® ROLLOMATIC E

Tooth

Chain

Hand guard

Back muffler

Front muffler

Needle
cage

Hand guard

Starter grip

Guide bar

Rear
handle

Chain

Clutch
sprocket

STIHL

STIHL

Spiked
bumper

Fan vent

Sprocket cover

Guide bar
nut

Front
handle

Mini television

MINIATURIZED TELEVISION SETS are small enough to be held in the hand while being watched. A signal sent by a broadcast transmitter is picked up by the television antenna and passed to an electron gun at the back of the television set. In response to the signal this gun produces an electron beam that is passed through a deflection yoke. The yoke contains magnets and coils that cause the beam to scan across the screen in a series of lines. The screen is coated with phosphor, which glows when hit by the beam. As the beam scans the screen, its strength is varied so that the phosphor glows with different intensities in different parts of the screen. A continuous sequence of 25 black-and-white pictures per second appears on the screen so rapidly that the illusion of a moving picture is created.

Antenna connector

Tuner

Rear cabinet

Electrolytic capacitor

Dial pointer

Tuning drive gear

Keystone (East-West) amplifier integrated circuit

CATHODE RAY TUBE (CRT)

CRT cover

Earphone jack

Direct current jack

Tuning dial

Metal shield

Tuning printed circuit board

Battery compartment

Screw

Deflection coil

CRT bracket

Battery case lid

Tape

Positive pole

Electron gun

Mounting bracket

TUBE NECK

Nipple

Scan coil clamp

BATTERY CONTACTS

SCAN COIL DEFLECTION YOKE

Connecting pin

CRT socket

Centering magnet

Positive pole

Negative pole

Positive pole

Screw

Intermediate frequency coil

PRINTED CIRCUIT BOARD

Choke

Antenna holder

Plastic sheath

Ornamental strip

Coil

Glue

Horizontal frequency adjustment

Capacitor

Volume control dial

Power switch

Power dial

Filter

Window

Fly back transformer

Plastic cap

Focus control

Extra-high tension lead

SONY

21 30 40 50 60 68 UHF

FD-250B

Speaker

Filter ornament

Front cabinet

Chair

A TRADITIONALLY MADE DINING CHAIR, such as the Regency-style carver shown here, is held together, not by nails or bolts, but by snugly fitting joints, screws, dowels, and glue. Its curved arms and top splats, as well as its tapering legs, are cut from seasoned—that is, dried—mahogany. Mortice slots in the back legs receive the tenon tongues of the top and bottom splats; angled grooves at the top of the back legs, called rebates, take the curved arm rail. Though the various joints are so tight-fitting that they could produce a solid frame on their own, screws and glue are used to give the joints added strength. The comfortable, upholstered seatpad shown here consists of a patterned cover, calico lining, and foam padding that has been treated for fire safety; it is supported by webbing stretched across a wood frame.

Top splat

Cross stick

Bottom splat

Arm

Head

Seatpad

Front rail

Back leg

Left front leg

Square brass line

Mortice

Tenon

Tenon

Arm

Washer

Groove

Top splat

Washer

Dowel screw

Diamond

Screw

Splat mortice

Screw

Wood plug

Wood plug

Head

Cross stick

Bottom splat

Tenon

Side rail

Dowel hole

Screw

Dowel

Back rail

Dowel

Dowel

Dowel

Right front leg

Back leg

Dowel

Dowel hole

Front rail

CHAIR FRAME

SEAT UPHOLSTERY

Seat cover

Mortice

Webbing

Arm

Foam padding

Calico lining

Dowel screw

Splat mortice

Head

Seat back rail

Tenon

Side rail

Dowel hole

Screw

Bottom lining

Tack

SEAT FRAME

Back leg

Seat side rail

Seat side rail

Dowel hole

Seat front rail

Left front leg

Food processor

A FOOD PROCESSOR MAKES QUICK WORK of preparing ingredients. Razor-sharp blades of different shapes cut, chop, shred, slice, grate, or mince while other attachments whisk, knead, mix, or juice. The machine is powered by an electric motor that turns a drive wheel connected to a drive belt. This belt rotates a drive shaft gear that spins a drive shaft at high speed. The drive shaft then turns the attachment that is mounted on it. Because the spinning blades are potentially dangerous, safety is an important feature of all food processors. Safety interlocks make it impossible to operate the machine unless the lid is securely fixed. The cook also cannot reach the blades when the machine is working and so must drop ingredients through the filling funnel or into the rotating tray of a wide feed tube.

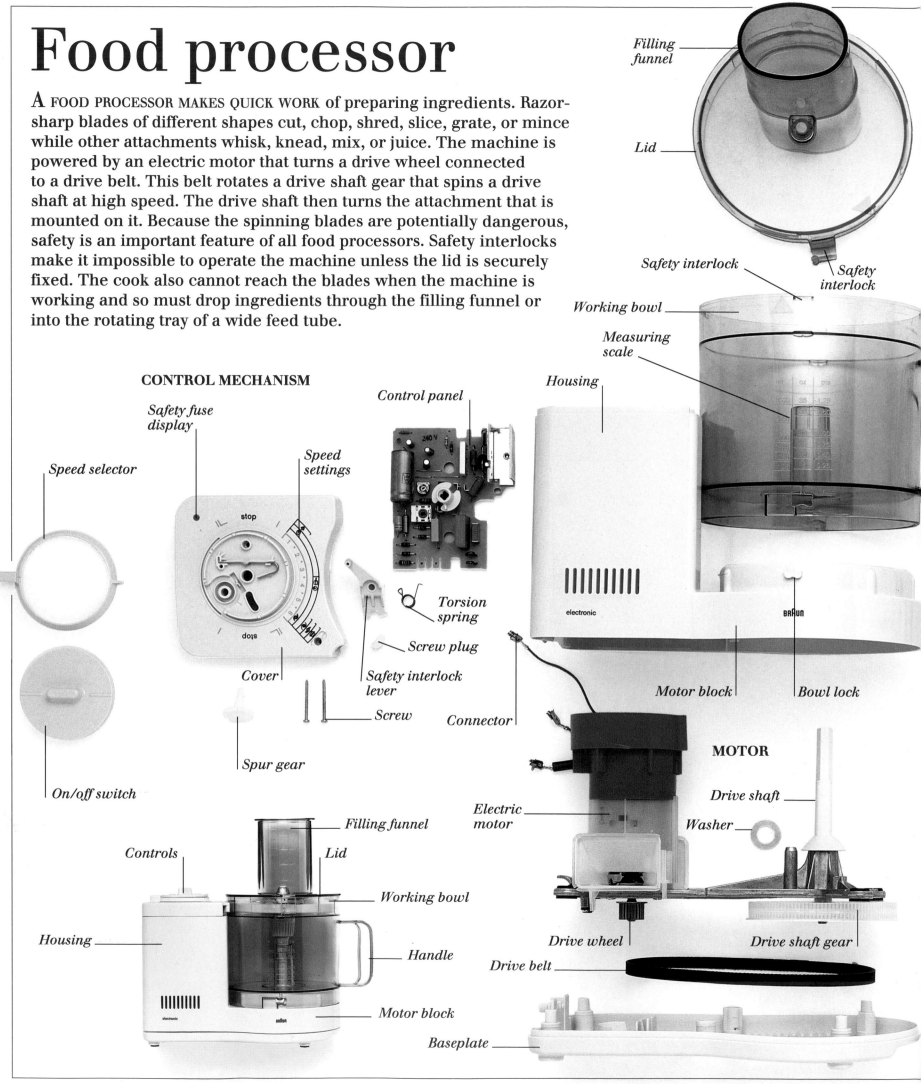

Filling funnel

Lid

Safety interlock

Safety interlock

Working bowl

Measuring scale

Housing

CONTROL MECHANISM

Safety fuse display

Speed selector

Control panel

Speed settings

stop

stop

Torsion spring

Screw plug

Cover

Safety interlock lever

Spur gear

Screw

Connector

On/off switch

Motor block

Bowl lock

MOTOR

Electric motor

Drive shaft

Washer

Controls

Filling funnel

Lid

Working bowl

Housing

Handle

Drive wheel

Drive shaft gear

Drive belt

Motor block

Baseplate

Pusher

Wide feed tube

Chopper handle

Tray

Blade insert

Safety interlock

Pusher and measuring cup

CAKE MIXER

Creaming bowl lid

SLICERS AND SHREDDERS

French fries cutter

Handle

Blade carrier

Coarse shredder

Slicer knob

Fine shredder

Adjusting knob holder

Whisk driving arm

Blade catch

Whisk

Dough hook

Slicer

Grater

Creaming and egg white bowl

Spatula

Baseplate screw

Foot

Typewriter

A TYPEWRITER IS A HAND-OPERATED printing machine. It has a set of keys marked with letters, figures, and other symbols. When the typist strikes a key with a finger, a system of levers or an electronic signal moves a raised version of the symbol, the type, toward an inked ribbon. The type may be on a series of bars or may be arranged around a sphere called a "golf ball." As the type makes contact, it prints an image of itself onto a sheet of paper held in position on the platen. A spring then moves the carriage and the paper forward a space. The next symbol can then be typed beside the first one.

Line spacing lever

Nut

Spring

C-clip

Line spacing linkage

Platen

MAINFRAME ASSEMBLY

Sub-frame

TYPEWRITER CASE

Baseplate

Ribbon spool

Segment slot

Type guide

Segment

Type bar link

Back space link

Type bar

Type

Keytop

Back space key

Shift lock key

Top plate

Shift key

Space bar

Margin rack

Platen

Paper release lever

Platen knob

Feed roll | Bail arm | **CARRIAGE** | Margin stop | Paper pan

Type bar

Keytop

Draw cord

Mainspring drumbox

Carriage sub-frame

Bolt

Ball bearing

Ball bearing holder

Shift link

Star wheel

Spring

Escapement dog

Escapement body

Nut

Screw

C-clip

Washer

Escapement wheel

Card holder

Back spacer link

Washer

Operating link

Ribbon carrier

RIBBON MECHANISM

Nut

Card scale

C-clip

Spring

Screw

Ribbon drive pawl

Ribbon

Type bar link

Ribbon drive link

Ribbon shaft

Spring

Type key lever

Spring

Ribbon drive

Ribbon spool

Suitcase

In the 19th century, wealthy people travelled abroad, they took their belongings in a series of specialized containers. Hats were in hatboxes, books and shoes and other general items were packed in trunks, and smart clothes for men were packed in flat valises, or suitcases. During this century, the flat suitcase has become the all-purpose travel bag, and good suitcases are designed to cope with all the potential problems of a long journey. The ideal suitcase has pockets for storing items such as shoes, and protects its contents from water, heat, humidity, sand, animals, and thieves.

Washer

Screw

Top corner piece

SUITCASE BODY

Metal fitting

Handle trim

Trim patch

Wire frame

Hardware buckle

Metal slider

Padlock

Webbing

Logo

Handle

Logo patch

Key

Webbing

Metal slider

Retractable pull-handle

Hardware buckle

Metal fitting

Handle trim

Body side

Trim patch

Body

Logo patch

Logo

Name tag

Trim patch

Webbing

Body side

Webbing

Handle

Name tag

Hardware buckle

Top corner piece

Screw

Washer

Corner piece

Interior strap

Zipper

Wheel

Trim patch

Washer

Webbing

Trim

Wheel cover

Washer

Screw

Screw

Security clasp

SUITCASE INTERIOR

Hardware buckle

Bottom board

Bottom stud

Metal frame

Bottom stud

Shoe pocket

Washer

Screw

Wire frame

Body

Interior zipper pocket

Webbing

Trim

Screw

Wheel cover

Washer

Security clasp

Hardware buckle

Wheel

Trim patch

Interior strap

Corner piece

Interior sheeting

Toaster

MOST ELECTRIC TOASTERS NOT ONLY GRILL slices of bread, they also pop them up when ready. While the slices rest on a spring-loaded rack, electric heating elements toast the bread. At the same time, a bimetallic strip heats and expands. One of the two metals in this strip expands more quickly than the other, causing the strip to curve. As it bends, it completes an electrical circuit and activates an electromagnet. The magnet attracts a catch, releasing the spring that holds the rack down in the toaster. The elements switch off, and the toasted slices pop up.

Terminal connections

Ejector bracket

Time switch

Variable time control knob

Selector switch

Screw

Screw

Switch end casting

Crumb tray

End baffle plate

Screw

Screw

Ground connection point

Cordset entry point

Foot

End element connecting link

End element

Baseplate

Screw

End element wire guard

Washer

Power supply cord

Bolt

Nut

Strain release

Ejector knob

Screw

Spring

Nut

Ejector bracket

Plain end casting

Switch end casting

Stainless steel cover

Selector switch

Ejector assembly

Ejector lever

Variable time control knob

Foot

Center element wire cage

Crumb tray

Inner cage assembly

Fixing screw

Screw

Foot

End baffle plate

Screw

Element retaining stop

Nut

Washer

Screw

Foot

Plain end casting

Screw

Stainless steel cover

Element connecting link

Center element

End element

Nut

Washer

Screw

End element wire guard

Umbrellas

Since ancient Egyptian times people have carried umbrellas to protect themselves from the weather. The first umbrellas were sunshades; the word comes from the Latin "umbra," which means "shadow." Today, an umbrella is usually a rain shelter, and a sunshade is called a parasol. Whatever the name, they work in the same way. A canopy of fabric is stretched over a frame of ribs. The ribs are attached to a runner, a short cylinder that encircles the central tube. When the runner is raised—either by hand, or automatically by springs—the canopy opens; when the runner is lowered—usually manually—the canopy collapses. Many automatic umbrellas have foldable ribs that enable them to collapse to about half the size of stick umbrellas.

AUTOMATIC COLLAPSIBLE FRAME

Main rib

Rib

Tip

UMBRELLA COVER

Stitching

Gore

Band

Press stud

Spreader wire

Runner wire

Lock spring

Runner wire

Washer

Runner

Top spring

Runner

Lock spring

Tip cup

Runner cover

AUTOMATIC COLLAPSIBLE UMBRELLA

Band

Tip

Handle

Cover

Release button

Handle

Handle

Release button

Screw

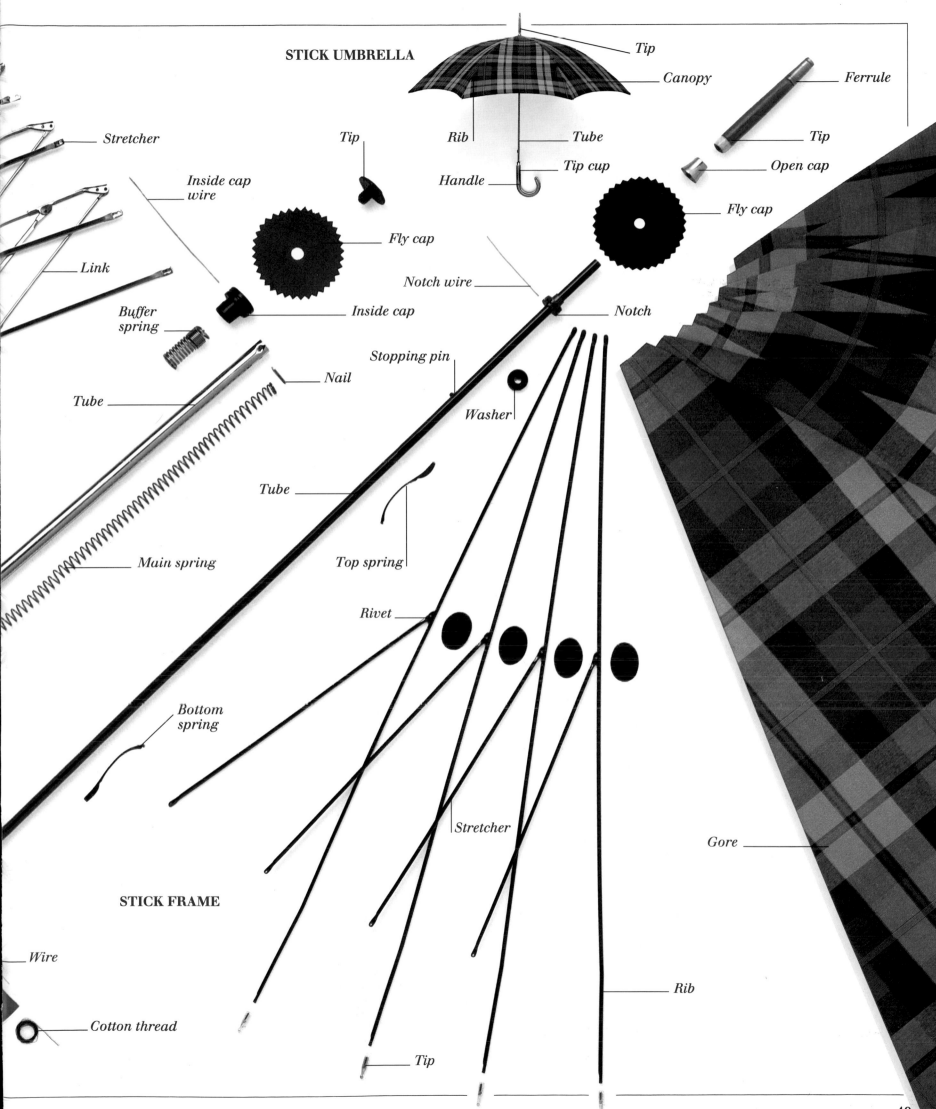

STICK UMBRELLA

Tip

Canopy

Ferrule

Rib

Tube

Tip

Stretcher

Tip

Handle

Tip cup

Open cap

Inside cap wire

Fly cap

Fly cap

Link

Notch wire

Buffer spring

Fly cap

Inside cap

Notch

Tube

Nail

Stopping pin

Washer

Tube

Top spring

Main spring

Rivet

Bottom spring

Stretcher

Gore

Wire

STICK FRAME

Rib

Cotton thread

Tip

Lawnmower

THE SHARP BLADES OF A LAWNMOWER—whether driven by electrical, gasoline, or human power—shave grass close to the ground. The gasoline-powered type shown here has a small engine that is electrically ignited by a battery and spark plug. This engine rotates a horizontal blade at the base of the lawnmower, which then slices the grass against a fixed blade. A grass bag at the back of the machine collects the cuttings. As the engine rotates the blades, it also turns the rear wheels, moving the lawnmower forward. Gears ensure that the horizontal blade spins faster than the wheels so that all of the grass is cut neatly before the lawnmower moves on.

Rear tire

Wheel cover

Rear wheel

GEAR CASE ASSEMBLY

Upper gear case

Wheel bolt

Blower shroud

Fuel tank

Drive shaft

Spring

Door

Half pulley

Belt guard

Drive belt

Screw

Cap

Screw

Door seal

Oil dipstick

Bolt

Oil fill tube

Screw

ENGINE AND RECOIL ASSEMBLY

Flywheel

Screw

OHV

Recoil case

Housing

Screw

Starter cup

Screw

Blade cover

Muffler cover

Throttle guard

Muffler

Engine pulley

Air filter

Screw

Height adjuster

Shoulder screw

Air filter cover

Front tire

Front wheel

53 cm

Handle

Control panel

Grass bag

Fuel tank cap

Recoil case

Muffler cover

Latch handle

Rear wheel

Housing

Front wheel

Handle

Mower drive handle

Traction lever

Throttle control lever

Ground speed control knob

Control lever

Traction cable support

Control panel

Battery

Vertical panel

Cable support bracket

Latch handle

Screen panel

Door discharge

Battery retainer

HANDLE AND TRACTION CONTROL ASSEMBLY

Grass bag

Traction cable

Blade

Screw

Blade retainer

Blade bolt

Washer

Grass bag frame

Battery connection

Wheel bolt

Saddle

THE FIRST HORSEBACK RIDERS HAD NO SADDLES; they sat bareback, clinging to the animal's mane. Next came a simple cloth saddle. The leather saddle, which was invented about 2,000 years ago by the warriors of the Asian steppes, revolutionized horseback riding. On this saddle, horsemen could gallop toward the enemy, fire arrows in all directions, and stay on their horses. Modern saddles are of two main types. The Western saddle is a heavy, working saddle used mainly by ranch hands in the United States. It has a metal horn at the front for securing a lasso and a high cantle at the back to keep the rider on the horse. The English saddle is much lighter. Designed for sport, it allows the horse to gallop fast. Its drawback is that it provides less stability; to stay on the horse, the rider must grip the animal with the knees.

ENGLISH SADDLE

Cantle
Leather seat
Pommel
Sloped head
Dee
Surcingle
Block flap
Girth
Stirrup leather
Stirrup

Facing
Strap bearing
Gullet
Web
Gullet plate
Point pocket
Tree
Stirrup bar
Stuffing hole
Cantle
Knee roll
Metal reinforcement
Web
Copper rivet
Top leather
Spring tree
Flexible leather point
Point cover
Facing
Rivet
Belly nail
Lining of underside of saddle
Knee cover
Brass nameplate nail
Tack
Gullet lining
Nylon rope
Screw
Stirrup buckle
Stirrup leather
Flock stuffing

SHAPED GIRTH

Girth buckle

Chape

Stirrup

Block flap

Buckle guard

Plated nail

Dee

Billet strap

Surcingle

Name-plate

Stirrup buckle

Bar leather

Belly nail

Forepiece

Dee

Skirt

Stirrup leather

Webbing

Welt

Back

Leather seat

Canvas

Canvas

Back

Leather

Rubber seat

Welt

Canvas

Skirt

Buckle guard

Belly nail

Bar leather

Lacing thread

3-cord linen thread

Surcingle

Nameplate

Leather belly

Beeswax

4-cord linen thread

Dee

Stirrup

Plated nail

Stirrup leather

Stirrup

Block flap

Espresso machine

AN ESPRESSO MACHINE MAKES the strong Italian coffee of the same name. It does this by forcing very hot water through dark-roasted, finely ground beans to extract their flavor. First, water is poured into the boiler tank until the correct level is reached (the water level can be seen in the sight glass). The machine is then switched on, and the element boils the water. When steam escapes through the steam release valve, the machine is ready to make coffee. The ground beans are measured into the filter, which rests in its holder, then the holder is slotted into the bottom of the group chamber, which channels hot water from the boiler to the coffee. A cup is placed under the spouts. The lever is then raised, opening a valve to let hot water enter the group chamber. Lowering the lever forces the hot water through the ground coffee, into the spouts, and finally into the cup. By placing a jug of milk under the steam tube and opening the steam tap, you can also heat and froth milk to make cappuccino coffee.

Steam tap

Boiler cap

Screw

Steam tap socket

BOILER TANK

Group socket

Washer

Boiler case

Nut

Sight glass

Sight glass holder

Washer

Nut

Sight glass bracket

Switch position

Live wire

Outer grommet

Large element

Neutral wire

Small element

Ground wire

Inner grommet

Washer

Heater screw

Lead wire

Baseplate

Positive wire

Negative wire

HEATER ELEMENT

STEAM RELEASE VALVE

Valve cap

Spring

Ball bearing

Steam release valve collar

Steam tube

Tube

Screw

Washer

Base

Maker's label

On/off switch

Fusible link

High/low pressure switch

Ground wire

Base screw socket

Top cap

Lock nut

GROUP

Bolt

Group tap

Group chamber

Group pipe

Filter plate

Filter

Steam jet

C-clip

Nut

Bolt

Lever

Lever handle

Coffee press

FILTER HOLDER

Handle

Spout

Measuring spoon

Drip grid

Drip tray

Lever handle

Lever

Steam tap

Group chamber

Steam tube

Handle

Boiler case

Spout

Sight glass tube

Sight glass bracket

Base

Drip grid

Trench coat

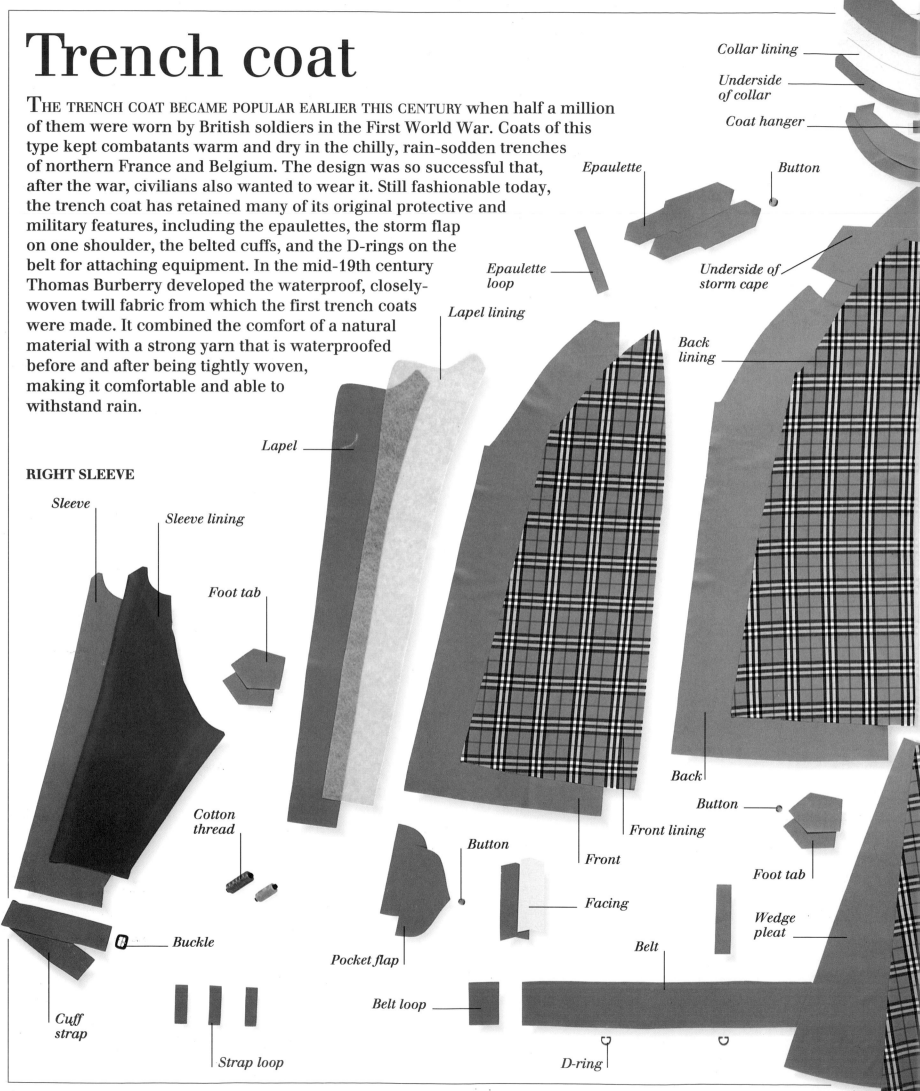

THE TRENCH COAT BECAME POPULAR EARLIER THIS CENTURY when half a million of them were worn by British soldiers in the First World War. Coats of this type kept combatants warm and dry in the chilly, rain-sodden trenches of northern France and Belgium. The design was so successful that, after the war, civilians also wanted to wear it. Still fashionable today, the trench coat has retained many of its original protective and military features, including the epaulettes, the storm flap on one shoulder, the belted cuffs, and the D-rings on the belt for attaching equipment. In the mid-19th century Thomas Burberry developed the waterproof, closely-woven twill fabric from which the first trench coats were made. It combined the comfort of a natural material with a strong yarn that is waterproofed before and after being tightly woven, making it comfortable and able to withstand rain.

RIGHT SLEEVE

Collar lining

Underside of collar

Coat hanger

Epaulette

Button

Epaulette loop

Underside of storm cape

Lapel lining

Back lining

Lapel

Sleeve

Sleeve lining

Foot tab

Cotton thread

Button

Back

Button

Front lining

Front

Foot tab

Facing

Wedge pleat

Pocket flap

Belt

Buckle

Belt loop

Cuff strap

Strap loop

D-ring

Top of collar

COLLAR

Welt

Epaulette

Epaulette loop

Storm flap

Button

Storm cape

Back lining

Storm flap

Cuff strap

Pocket flap

Button

Lapel lining

Back

Button

Button

Reinforcing button

Sleeve

LEFT SLEEVE

Wedge pleat lining

Front lining

Front

Button

Lapel

WEDGE

Pocket welt

Sleeve lining

Belt loop

Button

Belt

Pocket flap

Buckle

Buckle

Strap loop

Buckle

Cuff strap

Bicycle

BICYCLES ARE AMONG THE WORLD'S most popular forms of transport. The first pedal-driven bicycle was built in Scotland in 1839. Since then, the basic design has been gradually improved, with the addition of a chain, gears, and pneumatic tires. The recent invention of the mountain, or all-terrain, bike has been an important development. With its strong, rugged frame, wide tires, and 21 gears, the mountain bike shown here enables the rider to reach rough and hilly areas previously inaccessible to cyclists.

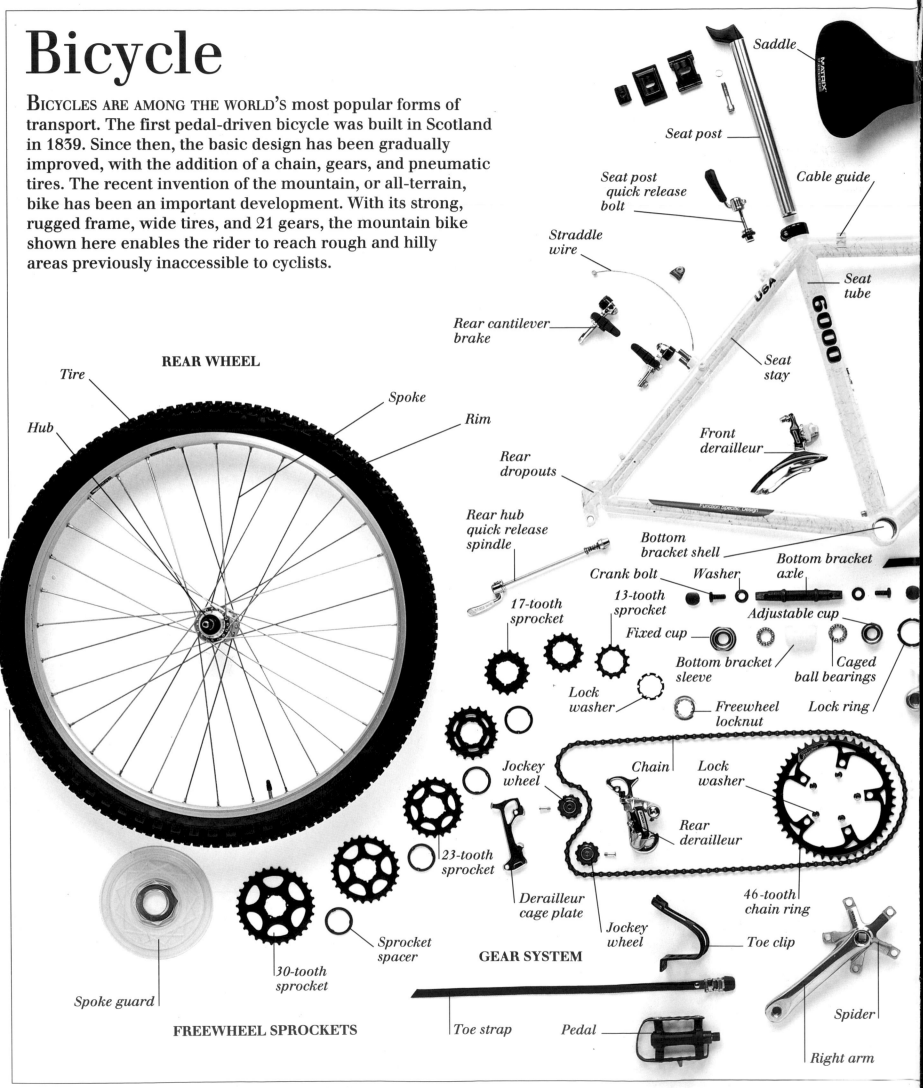

Saddle

Seat post

Seat post quick release bolt

Cable guide

Straddle wire

Rear cantilever brake

Seat tube

Seat stay

REAR WHEEL

Tire

Spoke

Rim

Hub

Front derailleur

Rear dropouts

Rear hub quick release spindle

Bottom bracket shell

Bottom bracket axle

Crank bolt   Washer

17-tooth sprocket

13-tooth sprocket

Adjustable cup

Fixed cup

Bottom bracket sleeve

Caged ball bearings

Lock ring

Lock washer

Freewheel locknut

Jockey wheel

Chain

Lock washer

Rear derailleur

23-tooth sprocket

Derailleur cage plate

Jockey wheel

46-tooth chain ring

Toe clip

Sprocket spacer

GEAR SYSTEM

30-tooth sprocket

Spoke guard

Spider

FREEWHEEL SPROCKETS

Toe strap

Pedal

Right arm

Gear cable

Gearshift

Handlebar stem

Gearshift

Handlebar

Handlebar grip

Expander bolt

Lock nut

Rear brake cable

Top tube

Brake lever

Brake lever

Top race

Lock washer

Cable guide

Head tube

Top cup

Caged ball bearings

Front brake cable

Hub

BICYCLE FRAME

Bottom cup

Rubber bearing seal

Spoke

Down tube

Straddle wire

Steerer tube

Bottom race

Toe clip

Front cantilever brake

Cantilever brake boss

Toe strap

Pedal

Rim

Left arm

Fork blade

Inner tube

24-tooth chain ring

Front hub quick release spindle

36-tooth chain ring

Handlebar

Saddle

Frame

Brake lever and gearshift

Valve cap

Valve

Pedal

Tire

FRONT WHEEL

Chain

Index

A

Aberdeen hook 18
Absorbent separator 16
Adjustable cup 58
Adjustable vane 19
Adjusting knob holder 41
Adjustment locking nut 33
Air exhaust slot 21
Air filter back 34
Air filter cover 50
Air filter front 34
Air intake slot 21
Air seal 17
Alarm reset button 14
Alkaline manganese power
    cell 16
Alkaline power cell 17
All terrain bike 58
Amplifier 14
Anatomy of a hook 18
Angle 32
Anode 16-17
Anode cap 17
Anode collector 17
Antenna 36
Antenna connector 36
Antenna holder 37
Anti-reverse device 18
Aperture 28
Aperture auto-lock
    button 29
Aperture/distance index 29
Arch 22
Arm
    Bicycle 58-59
    Chair 38
    Teddy bear 30
Armature 20
Armature spindle 20
Arm coupling 33
Arm disk 31
Arm rail 38
Arm swivel joint system 31
Artificial flies 18-19
Artificial lures 18-19
Automatic collapsible
    frame 48
Automatic collapsible
    umbrella 48
Auto-stop lever 15

B

Back
    Saddle 53
    Suit 8-9
    Trench coat 56-57
Back box 7
Back cover 28
Back cover board
    Half-bound book 27
    Leather-bound book 27
Back curtain 9
Back leg 38-39
Back lining
    Shoe 23
    Suit 8-9
    Trench coat 56-57
Back plate 7
Back rail 38
Back space key 42
Back space link 42-43
Bail arm
    Fixed-spool reel 18
    Typewriter 43
Bait 18
Ball 12-13

Ball bearing
    Espresso machine 55
    Typewriter 43
Ball bearing holder 43
Ballpoint 13
Ballpoint pen 12-13
Band
    Automatic collapsible
        umbrella 48
    Umbrella cover 48
Barb 18
Bar leather 53
Barrel
    Ballpoint pen 12-13
    Fountain pen 13
    Mechanical pencil 12
Barrel arbor hook 6
Barrel band 13
Barrel pivot hole 6
Barrel swivel 18
Barrier separator 17
Base
    Espresso machine 55
    Telephone 11
Base casing 11
Baseplate
    Espresso machine 54
    Food processor 40
    Toaster 46
    Typewriter 42
Baseplate screw 41
Base screw socket 55
Batteries 16-17
Battery
    Camera 28
    Lawnmower 50-51
Battery case lid 36
Battery chamber cap 28
Battery compartment 36
Battery connection 51
Battery contact 36
Battery cover 16
Battery level indicator 24-25
Battery retainer 51
Beam 36
Beardtrimmer 24-25
Bearing 21
Beeswax 53
Belly nail 52-53
Belt 56-57
Belt clip 14
Belted cuff 56
Belt guard 50
Belt loop
    Suit 8
    Trench coat 56-57
Bespoke suit 8
Bicycle 58-59
Bicycle frame 58-59
Billet strap 53
Bimetallic strip 46
Blade
    Cut-throat razor 24
    Food processor 40
    Lawnmower 50-51
Blade bolt 51
Blade carrier 41
Blade catch 41
Blade cover 50
Blade guard 24
Blade insert 41
Blade retainer 51
Blade screen comb 24
Block flap 52-53
Blower shroud 50
Body
    Deer hopper dry fly 19
    Lamp 32
    Suitcase 44
    Teddy bear 30

Body back 31
Body covering 28
Body disk 31
Body front 31
Body side 44
Boiler cap 54
Boiler case 54-55
Boiler tank 54
Bolt
    Espresso machine 55
    Lawnmower 50
    Toaster 46
    Typewriter 43
Bookbinding 26
Books 26-27
Bottom board 45
Bottom bracket axle 58
Bottom bracket shell 58
Bottom bracket sleeve 58
Bottom cover 28
Bottom cover assembly 28
Bottom cup 59
Bottom door 7
Bottom door key 7
Bottom filler 22-23
Bottom lining 39
Bottom race 59
Bottom splat 38
Bottom spring 49
Bottom stud 45
Bowl lock 40
Box toe 22
Brace-and-bit 20-21
Brace button 8
Bracket
    Electric shaver 24
    Lamp 32
Bracket shell 58
Brake lever 59
Brass buckle 30
Brass nameplate nail 52
Bread 46
Breast pocket 9
Bridge 7
Bridge screw 7
Broadcast transmitter 36
Brush 20
Brush holder 20
Brush spring 20
Buckle 56-57
Buckle guard 53
Buckram corner piece 26-27
Buffer spring 49
Bushing 32-33
Butt cap 19
Butt extension 19
Button
    Suit 8-9
    Trench coat 56-57
Button cell 17
Button hole silk 9
Butt section 18-19

C

Cabinet front cover 15
Cabinet rear cover 14
Cable cordset 20
Cable guide 58-59
Cable support bracket 51
Cadmium anode 17
Caged ball bearings 58-59
Cake mixer 41
Calico 38
Calico lining 38-39
Camera 28-29
Cannon pinion 7
Canopy 48-49

Cantilever brake boss 59
Cantle 52
Canvas
    Saddle 53
    Suit 8-9
Cap
    Lamp 32
    Lawnmower 50
    Mechanical pencil 12
Capacitor
    Electric shaver 25
    Mini television 37
    Telephone 11
Cap nut 32
Cappuccino coffee 54
Capstan 14
Capstan belt 15
Car battery 16
Carbon 12
Carbon contact 10
Carburetor 34
Carburetor box cover 34
Card holder 43
Card scale 43
Carriage 42-43
Carriage sub-frame 43
Carry case 14
Case
    Books 26
    Safety razor 24
Case exterior 25
Case interior 25
Case screw 25
Cassette 14
Cassette holder clamper 14
Cassette holder click arm
    assembly 14
Cassette window 14-15
Cathode 16-17
Cathode cap 17
Cathode collector 16
Cathode ray tube 36
C-clip
    Espresso machine 55
    Typewriter 42-43
Cell case 17
Cell divider 17
Cell top 17
Center element 47
Center element wire cage
    47
Center hole 7
Centering magnet 36
Center wheel 6
Centrifugal brake 18
Chain
    Bicycle 58-59
    Chainsaw 34-35
Chain brake 34
Chain ring 58-59
Chainsaw 34-35
Chair 38-39
Chair frame 38
Chair rail 38
Chape 53
Charge lamp 24-25
Chassis 14
Chassis assembly 15
Check pawl 18
Check pawl cover 18
Check slide 18
Check spring 18
Cheek 19
Cheese head screw 33
Choke 37
Chopper handle 41
Chuck
    Brace-and-bit 21
    Hand drill 21
    Power drill 21

Chuck key 21
Chuck key holder 20-21
Chuck key pilot hole 21
Clamping screw 33
Clamp lower jaw 33
Clamp upper jaw 33
Clay 12
Cleaning wire 12
Clicker plate 19
Click mechanism 18
Click wheel 6
Clip
    Ballpoint pen 12-13
    Fountain pen 13
    Mechanical pencil 12
Clip screw 13
Clip screw bush 13
Clock 6-7
    Personal stereo 14
Clock case 6
Clock face 7
Clock retainer plate shield 15
Clock train 6
Cloth
    Books 26
    Suit 8
Clutch
    Fountain pen 13
    Mechanical pencil 12
    Personal stereo 15
Clutch sprocket 34-35
Coarse shredder 41
Coat hanger 56
Cock screw 7
Coffee press 55
Coil 36-37
Coil tension spring 33
Coin pocket 8
Collar
    Safety razor 24
    Suit 8-9
    Trench coat 57
Collar canvas 9
Collar lining 56
Collector
    Ballpoint pen 13
    Fountain pen 13
Collector shell 13
Collet retainer 12
Comfort control 24
Commutator 20
Cone
    Last 23
    Personal stereo 14
Connecting pin 36
Connecting wire 32
Connector
    Ballpoint pen 13
    Food processor 40
    Fountain pen 13
Control lever
    Chainsaw 34
    Lawnmower 51
Control mechanism 40
Control panel 51
Controls 40
Converter 13
Copper conductor 32
Cord
    Personal stereo 15
    Telephone 11
Cordset entry point 46
Corner piece
    Half-bound book 26
    Suitcase 44-45
Cotton thread
    Stick frame 48-49
    Trench coat 56
Counter 22-23
Counter dial cover 29

Counter dial housing 29
Counter stiffener 23
Cover
    Automatic collapsible
        umbrella 48
    Books 26
    Food processor 40
Cover board 26
Cover frame 29
Cradle switch 11
Cradle switch assembly 11
Cradle switch lever 11
Crank 21
Crank bolt 58
Creaming and egg white
    bowl 41
Creaming bowl lid 41
Cross section of a button
    cell 17
Cross section of finished
    shoe 22
Cross stick 38
CRT 36
CRT bracket 36
CRT cover 36
CRT socket 36
Crumb tray 46-47
Crutch 6
Crutch screw 6
Cuff 22
Cuff button 8-9
Cuff button facing 8-9
Cuff lining 8-9
Cuff strap 56-57
Current 16
Cutter 24
Cut-throat razor 24
Cylinder 36

D

Date button 14-15
Decorative plastic trim 10
Dee 52-53
Deer hopper dry fly 19
Deflection coil 36
Deflection yoke 36
Depth-of-field guide 29
Derailleur cage plate 58
Devon minnow 19
Dial 7
Dial foot hole 7
Dial pointer 36
Dial washer 7
Diamond 38
Diaphragm
    Camera 28
    Telephone 10
Diaphragm blade 29
Dining chair 38
Diode 11
Direct current jack 36
Disk 30-31
Disk drag 18
Disk drag housing 19
Disk spring 18
Display holder 15
Dome 32
Door 50
Door discharge 51
Door seal 50
Double-edged blade 24
Dough hook 41
Dowel 38
Dowel hole 38-39
Dowel screw 38-39
Down tube 59
Drag adjustment 18

Drag knob 19
Drag knob screw 19
Drag spindle 18
Drag washer 18
Draw cord 43
Drill bit
  Brace-and-bit 21
  Hand drill 21
  Power drill 21
Drills 20-21
D-ring 56
Drip grid 55
Drip tray 55
Drive belt
  Food processor 40
  Lawnmower 50
Drive cog 34
Drive handle 51
Drive shaft
  Electric shaver 24
  Food processor 40
  Lawnmower 50
Drive shaft gear 40
Drive wheel
  Food processor 40
  Hand drill 21
Dual click gear 18
Dunkeld wet fly 19
Dustcover for earpiece 10
Dustcover for mouthpiece 10

E

Ear 30
Ear back 30
Ear front 30
Earphone 14-15
Earphone jack 36
Earpiece 10
Earpiece transducer 10
East-West amplifier
  integrated circuit 36
E-clip 34
Ejector assembly 47
Ejector bracket 46-47
Ejector lever 47
Electrical circuit 46
Electrically driven motor 34
Electrical signal 10
Electric current 14
Electric motor 40
Electric shaver 24
Electric toaster 46
Electrolyte 16
Electrolytic capacitor 36
Electromagnet
  Telephone 10
  Toaster 46
Electromagnetic induction
  capacitor 20
Electron beam 36
Electron flow 16
Electron gun 36
Electronic signal 42
Element retaining stop 47
End baffle plate 46-47
End cap 32-33
End element 46-47
End element connecting link
  46-47
End element wire
  guard 46-47
Endpaper
  Half-bound book 26-27
  Leather-bound book 27
Engine 50
Engine and recoil
  assembly 50

Engine pulley 50
English saddle 52
Epaulette 56-57
Epaulette loop 56-57
Eraser 12
Escapement body 43
Escapement dog 43
Escape wheel 6
Espresso machine 54-55
Exchange number 11
Expander bolt 59
Exposure 28
Exposure counter 28-29
Exposure counter dial 29
Extra-high tension lead 37
Eye
  Anatomy of a hook 18
  Deer hopper dry fly 19
  Devon minnow 19
  Nib 13
  Teddy bear 30
Eyelet 22-23

F

Fabric 48
Facing
  Saddle 52
  Suit 9
  Trenchcoat 56
Facing of lapel 8-9
Fan 20
Fan housing 34
Fan vent 35
Fanwheel 34
Fastening 8
Fast-forward and rewind
  pulley assembly 15
Fast-forward button 14
Fast-forward gear 15
Feed 13
Feed roll 43
Feed tube 40
Felt 30
Female lead connector 14
Ferrule 49
Field 20
Filament 32
Filler unit
  Ballpoint pen 13
  Fountain pen 13
Filling funnel 40
Film 28
Film chamber 28
Film guide rail 28
Film pressure plate 28
Film rail 28
Film rewind/back cover
  release knob 28-29
Film rewind crank 28-29
Film roller 28
Film speed indicator 29
Film sprocket spool 28
Film take-up spool 28
Film wind lever 29
Filter
  Espresso machine 55
  Mini television 37
Filter holder 55
Filter ornament 37
Filter plate 55
Fin 19
Fine shredder 41
Fire safety 38
Fishing tackle 18-19
Fixed cup 58
Fixed-spool reel 18
Fixing screw 47

Flashgun 28
Flexible leather point 52
Flock stuffing 52
Fly back transformer 37
Fly button 9
Fly cap
  Automatic collapsible
    frame 48-49
  Stick frame 48-49
Flyleaf 27
Fly reel 18-19
Fly rod 18-19
Flywheel
  Chainsaw 34
  Lawnmower 50
Foam padding 38-39
Focus control 37
Focusing ring 29
Food processor 40-41
Foot
  Food processor 41
  Toaster 46-47
Footpad 31
Footpad reinforcement 31
Foot tab 56
Fore edge
  Half-bound book 26
  Leather-bound book 27
Forepart 8 0
Forepart lining 8-9
Forepiece 53
Fork blade 59
Fountain pen 12-13
Frame 59
Freewheel locknut 58
Freewheel sprocket 58
French bearer 9
French fries cutter 41
Front 56-57
Front board assembly 28
Front brake cable 59
Front cabinet 37
Front cantilever brake 59
Front cover board
  Half-bound book 26
  Leather-bound book 27
Front derailleur 58
Front hackle 19
Front handle 35
Front hub quick release
  spindle 59
Frontispiece 27
Front leg
  Chair 38-39
  Suit 8
Front lens frame retainer
  plate 28
Front lens group 28
Front lining 56-57
Front plate 6
Front rail 38
Front tire 50
Front wheel
  Bicycle 59
  Lawnmower 50-51
Fuel filler cap 34
Fuel tank 50
Fuel tank cap 51
Function button seal 14
Fusee 6
Fusee chain 6
Fuse enclosure 32
Fusee pivot hole 6
Fusee stop 6
Fusee stop screw 6
Fusible link 55

G

Gallop 52
Gape 18
Garment 8
Gasoline-driven motor 34
Gear 40
Gear cable 59
Gearcase 21
Gearcase assembly 50
Gearcase cover 21
Gearcase cover screw 21
Gearcase position 20
Gearcase screw 21
Gear cover 24
Gear frame 24
Gearing system 18
Gear mechanism 21
Gear retainer 18
Gears
  Clock 6
  Drills 20
  Lawnmower 50
Gearshift 59
Gear system
  Bicycle 58
  Electric shaver 24
Gear wheel 24
Gimp 0
Girth 52
Girth buckle 53
Glass envelope 32
Glue
  Books 26
  Chair 38
  Mini television 37
Gold tooling 26-27
Golfball 42
Gore 48-49
Graphite 12
Graphite pencil 12
Grass bag 51
Grass bag frame 51
Grater 41
Groove 38
Ground coffee 54
Ground connection
  point 46
Ground speed control
  knob 51
Ground wire 54-55
Group 55
Group chamber 54-55
Group pipe 55
Group socket 54
Group tap 55
Guide 8
Guide bar 34-35
Guide bar nut 35
Gullet 52
Gullet lining 52
Gullet plate 52

H

Hackle 19
Half-bound book 26
Half pulley 50
Hammer actuator
  position 20
Hammer mechanism 20
Hammer mechanism
  actuator 20-21
Hand-bound book 26
Hand collet 7
Hand drill 20-21
Handgrip 18
Hand guard 34-35

Handle
  Automatic collapsible
    frame 48-49
  Automatic collapsible
    umbrella 48
  Brace-and-bit 21
  Cut-throat razor 24
  Espresso machine 55
  Fixed-spool reel 18
  Fly reel 19
  Food processor 40-41
  Lawnmower 51
  Multiplier reel 18
  Safety razor 24
  Stick frame 48-49
  Stick umbrella 49
  Suitcase 44
  Umbrella 48-49
Handle and traction control
  assembly 51
Handlebar 59
Handlebar grip 59
Handlebar stem 59
Handle trim 44
Handset 11
Handset back cover 11
Handset cord 11
Handset cord plug 11
Handset front cover 10
Hardback book 26
Hardware buckle 45
Hardware buckle catch 44
Head
  Brace-and-bit 21
  Chair 38-39
  Deer hopper dry fly 19
  Dunkeld wet fly 19
  Teddy bear 30
Headband
  Half-bound book 26
  Leather-bound book 27
Headphone jack 14
Headphone socket
  packing 14
Headset 15
Head tube 59
Hearing aid 16
Heater element 54
Heater screw 54
Heel
  Nib 13
  Shoes 22-23
Heel grip 22
Heel nail 23
Height adjuster 50
Hexagon nut
  Chainsaw 34
  Lamp 33
High/low pressure switch 55
Hillman anti-kink weight 18
Hinge 23
Hinged brass bezel 7
Hip flap pocket 9
Hole
  Camera 29
  Telephone 11
Hook 18-19
Horizontal frequency
  adjustment 37
Hot shoe 29
Hour hand 7
Hour hand screw 7
Hour marker 7
Hour wheel 7
Housing
  Food processor 40
  Lawnmower 50-51
Housing cover 20-21
Housing cover screw 21
Hub 58-59

I

Ignition module 34
Ink 12
Ink tube 13
Inlet 25
Inner cage assembly 47
Inner cap 13
Inner grommet 54
Inner sock 22-23
Inner tube 59
Inside cap 49
Inside cap wire 49
Inside pocket 8
Inside quarter 22
Insole 22
Insole with ribbing 23
Installing ring 29
Installing ring retainer
  plate 28
Insulating seal ring 17
Insulation 32
Integrated circuit 11
Interior sheeting 45
Interior strap 45
Interior zipper pocket 45
Intermediate frequency
  coil 37
Intermediate ring 19
Internal battery cover 15
Iridium tip 13

J

Jacket 8
Jacket button 8
Jacket hanger 8
Jack-locating hole 23
Jaw
  Brace-and-bit 21
  Hand drill 21
  Power drill 21
Jockey wheel 58
Joint
  Chair 38
  Jointed plug 19
  Leather-bound book 26-27
Jointed plug 19
Jointer 14

K

Keeper ring 18
Key
  Suitcase 44
  Typewriter 42
Key pad casing 10
Key pad contact 11
Key pad membrane 10
Keystone amplifier
  integrated circuit 36
Key top
  Telephone 10
  Typewriter 42-43
Knee cover 52
Knee roll 52

L

Lacing thread 53
Lamp 32-33
Lamp holder 32
Lamp holder coupling 33
Lapel 56-57

Washer (continued)
  Camera 28-29
  Chainsaw 34
  Chair 38
  Electric shaver 24
  Espresso machine 54-55
  Food processor 40
  Lamp 33
  Lawnmower 51
  Personal stereo 15
  Power drill 20-21
  Stick frame 48-49
  Suitcase 44-45
  Teddy bear 30-31
  Telephone 11
  Toaster 46-47

Typewriter 43
Web 52
Webbing
  Chair 38-39
  Saddle 53
  Suitcase 44
Wedge 57
Wedge pleat 56
Wedge pleat lining 57
Weight 18
Welt
  Saddle 53
  Shoes 22-23
  Trench coat 57
Western saddle 52
Wheel 45

Wheel bolt 50-51
Wheel cover
  Lawnmower 50
  Suitcase 45
Whisk 41
Whisk driving arm 41
Wide feed tube 41
Winding hole 7
Winding key 6
Wind lever collar 29
Wind lever install
  spring 29
Window
  Camera 29
  Mini television 37
  Telephone 10

Wing
  Deer hopper dry fly 19
  Nib 13
Wing cap 22
Wing cap and vamp lining 22
Wing cap backer 22
Wing nut 32-33
Wire
  Personal stereo 14
  Telephone 11
Wire frame 44-45
Wire spring 25
Wood 12
Wood bezel 7
Wood frame 38
Wood mold 22

Wood peg 6-7
Wood plug 38
Wood stick 12
Wood wool 30
Wood wool stuffing 30-31
Working bowl 40
Working saddle 52
Worklamp 32

X

X-contact 29
X-flash sync cap 28
X-flash sync terminal 28

Y

Yarn 56
Yoke 36

Z

Zinc air button cell 17
Zinc gel anode 17
Zipper 45

Acknowledgments

Dorling Kindersley would like to thank:
Active Clock Repair; City Clocks (Clocks); Agnews Tailors; Hacket; Paul Stewart (Suit); Audioline Ltd; S A Jackson; Precision Interconnect (Telephone); Arthur Brown & Co. Inc.; Berol Ltd; Parker Pen Co; Penfriend (London) Ltd; Philip Poole & Co Ltd; Rotring UK Ltd (Pencils and pens); Christopher Cullen, Babber Electronics; Golan Harris; Sony UK Ltd (Personal stereo; Mini television); Duracell International Inc.; Exide Batteries Ltd (Batteries); Capitol Fishing Tackle; Farlows of Pall Mall; House of Hardy; Leeda Fishing Tackle (Fishing tackle); Black and Decker Inc. (Drills); British Footwear Manufacturing Federation; Grenson Shoes Ltd; Joe's Shoe Repair (Shoes); Norelco Consumer Products; Philips Domestic Appliances and Personal Care (Shavers and razors); Distinctive Book Binders; The Folio Society; RS Book Binders (Books);

The Pentax Co. (Camera); Canterbury Bears Ltd; Pamela Thomas (Teddy bear); American Lighting Co.; F E Murdin, Decorative Lighting Association; Habitat (Lamp); Stihl (Chainsaw); Chingford Reproductions Ltd; Henredon (Chair); Braun Inc. (Food processor); Allens Typewriters Ltd; American Business Machines; W A Beeching; G F Currill (Typewriter); Carlton UK Ltd; US Leather & Luggage Co. (Suitcase); Black & Decker Inc.; Dualit Ltd (Toaster); Fulton Umbrellas Ltd; Sol Schaverien & Sons Ltd; Zip Jack Umbrellas (Umbrellas); J B Dove; Elmco; Toro Wheelhorse UK Ltd (Lawnmower); W&H Gidden Ltd; Miller Harness Co. (Saddle); European Gift & Houseware; Fairfax Engineering Ltd; Pavoni SPA (Espresso machine); Burberry's of London; London Town Corporation (Trench coat); Emey's Bicycles; F W Evans Cycles Ltd; Trek UK Ltd (Bicycle).

Additional design assistance:
Sandra Archer, Paul Calver, Simone End, Nicki Liddiard

Additional editorial assistance:
Susan Bosanko, Deirdre Clark, Edwina Johnson, Gail Lawther, Christine Murdock

Index:
Elaine Mills